lofts

living in space

lofts

living in space

orianna fielding banks
and **rebecca tanqueray**

special photography by Michael Harding

UNIVERSE

First published in the United States of America in 1999
by UNIVERSE PUBLISHING
A Division of Rizzoli International Publications, Inc.
300 Park Avenue South
New York, NY 10010

01 02 03 / 10 9 8 7 6 5 4 3 2

Printed in Dubai

Library of Congress Catalog Card Number: 99-71240
ISBN: 0-7893-0361-2

The authors and publisher have made every effort to ensure
that all financial information is correct and up to date at
the time of publication. Since it is common practice in the
UK and USA to describe the dimensions of property in
imperial measurements, these have been given first,
with metric conversions following.

contents

introduction

When loft-living first emerged in New York in the 1940s, it didn't look set to take the world by storm. Carving living spaces out of disused industrial buildings was very much a fringe fashion, a way for artists and designers to live and work in the city without being crippled by exorbitant rents. But what began as a radical alternative to conventional accommodation was to change the face of contemporary urban housing worldwide.

Fifty or so years since those first, few, very unrefined warehouse conversions, the loft – in its many guises – has spread right across the Western hemisphere, from Sydney to Stockholm, Chicago to Antwerp. The loft has become the fashionable residence of the day; a symbol of millennial cool; the aspirational interior for style-conscious home-owners everywhere.

How, you may be wondering, has the loft made the leap from bohemian refuge to des res with a widespread appeal? It has happened in stages, of course. While, at first, inhabiting a loft was absolutely not done if you had an ounce of class (imagine living in a factory, darling), it didn't take

**With sweeping floors,
high ceilings and vast
amounts of space and
light, the loft has become
the aspirational interior
of the millennium.**

long for the establishment to be seduced by the rough-around-the-edges kudos of this unconventional lifestyle and, with the help of forward-thinking developers and architects, for lofts to seep into the mainstream.

The image of the loft was – and still is – a major selling point. While its bohemian origins lent it a good dose of street cred, its portrayal on film further consolidated its appeal. We were wooed by Richard Bohringer's surreal warehouse in cult French film *Diva* (1981); then there was Charlie Sheen in *Wall Street* (1987), Demi Moore in *Ghost* (1990) and countless others. In the public imagination, lofts quickly became the territory of the cool, successful and beautiful, where everyone who was anyone wanted to live.

Image alone could not have sustained the massive growth of loft development that we have seen in the past few years. There is something in the very nature of the spaces themselves that strikes a chord in the consciousness of cosmopolitan people worldwide. Quite simply, the loft seems to be the perfect living space for modern life; a new kind of home for a new set of end-of-the-century needs. It is based in the city centre (no more commuting), uses recycled space (so we can be stylish and green) and, most important of all, offers what little other residential property can: serious amounts of unadulterated space and light.

Another winning attribute is its flexibility. Unlike most property, which comes with a ready-made internal layout, the loft offers a blank canvas that allows us the freedom to create exactly the kind of home we want, unconstrained by existing structures or features. We can leave the space open; divide it up; give it our individual aesthetic. As we define ourselves more and more through our interior decor, the loft has become the ultimate vehicle for self-expression.

It is not surprising, then, that the loft now appeals not just to artists but to a broad sweep of style-conscious city dwellers, and often those, ironically, with very pragmatic jobs. Alongside photographers, fashion designers and film directors are just as many bankers, lawyers and accountants who, relishing the chance to be creative at home, have bought into the lifestyle and helped to make the loft the most diverse of contemporary habitats. Raw or refined, rigorously minimal or softly modern; supremely tasteful or outrageously kitsch, the loft has the potential to be all things to all people.

Not only has the loft itself become urban society's most sought-after living space, it has also engendered a brand new aesthetic – the 'loft look' – which is making waves throughout the interiors world. In conventional houses, walls are being knocked down to create more space, light and flexibility; traditionally industrial, utilitarian materials – from stainless steel to scaffolding – are becoming the new domestic must-haves; and furniture is evolving to embrace forms that are versatile, informal and not room-dependant.

The loft, it seems, is liberating us from traditional notions of the home and conventional approaches to decoration. It has broadened the parameters of interior style and brought us unprecedented decorative freedom. It has given us a new-found confidence to do what we like with our homes, not what we should. But, most important of all, it has brought us, at long last, a way of living in the city and loving it.

Even the rawest space can become a sensual home. Here, a suede-edged fur blanket against a white waffle sheet make for a soft, modern bedroom.

1

the history

how it all began
crossing the atlantic
the london movement
the loft today

The loft has grown **gradually**, surreptitiously and **organically** from a marginal **bohemian** retreat into the **aspirational** home of the millennium.

how it all began

Loft-living started in mid-twentieth century New York, when artists began to occupy entire floors of derelict light-industrial factories in lower Manhattan, especially in SoHo, and turn them into living and work spaces. It is easy to see what motivated them. The districts of the city they had previously inhabited, such as Greenwich Village, were becoming increasingly popular and rents were escalating; moving into these unoccupied buildings in less appealing areas made good financial sense and, if they did it collectively, they could keep any conversion costs down.

Artists were drawn to these industrial-scale ex-factories for professional reasons, too. High ceilings. Vast open floor space. Giant windows. Where else could you find such perfect ingredients for a studio? These spaces had enough room to house vast works of art, there were freight lifts for transporting tools and materials and, most important of all, the quality of light was unbeatable. Adopting the kind of creative lifestyle that had been established a century earlier in the artists' ateliers of nineteenth-century Paris, New York's art crowd began to migrate to these buildings en masse.

Raw, unrefined and full of the grit and grime of their industrial past, these 'lofts' went against every conventional notion of the home. They were not cosy. They were not comfortable.

They were tough, primitive and unforgiving; qualities that the early dwellers did not have the money (nor, perhaps, the desire) to change. To keep costs down, they would do the absolute minimum to make the space habitable, leaving the bare bones of the building (the pipes, the beams, the bricks) exposed, unwittingly engendering the crude industrial look that was ultimately to become one of the key attractions of the loft.

Home comforts aside, these pioneering loft dwellers did not have an easy time of it. Town planners frequently refused to grant residential status to ex-industrial buildings so the occupants were sometimes forced to pay commercial rates or even evicted unless they devised clever ways of hiding the fact that their loft was more than just a work space. As a consequence, they designed stow-away sleeping areas, beds on pulleys, furniture on wheels; the kind of designs which have become integral to today's loft aesthetic but which then were simply a necessity. To give them clout against the

A hang-out for New York's alternative artists and musicians in the 1960s, Andy Warhol's The Factory did much to shape the loft's bohemian image.

reactionary urban authorities, the first loft occupiers tended to buy buildings (if they could) collectively, which also meant they could save money bulk-buying materials for the conversion. Turned into what were essentially artistic communes, these new 'loft buildings' soon became the territory of New York's avant-garde and anti-establishment and, in the 1960s, home to the movers and shakers of the music and modern art scenes. By the time Andy Warhol set up The Factory at 231 East 47th Street in November 1963 and started producing ground-breaking records with Lou Reed and the Velvet Underground, loft-living had become a bohemian cult.

It did not remain a fringe thing for long, however. Fairly soon the professional middle classes began to be attracted by the cool, streetwise associations of the loft and its affordability and began to adopt the lifestyle themselves, populating districts and buildings that had once been the sole preserve of the city's artists. The original art crowd, in turn, moved further south to an area called TriBeCa, and so the loft phenomenon spread further afield. Soon, responding to the growing demand for such living spaces, the New York authorities legalized the option to change some of the city's existing industrial stock to residential or mixed use. In the 1970s, recognizing the widespread appeal of these old warehouse buildings, they even listed parts of SoHo as enclaves of historic importance, confirming the entrance of lofts to the New York mainstream.

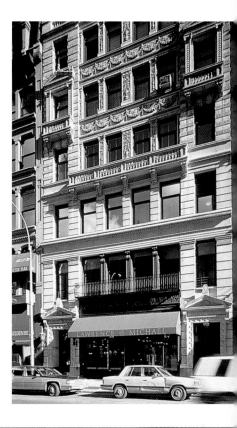

The loft has come a long way since the first raw industrial spaces. Today, behind original nineteenth-century facades, you are more likely to find highly designed interiors, such as this sleek and colourful modern space in London.

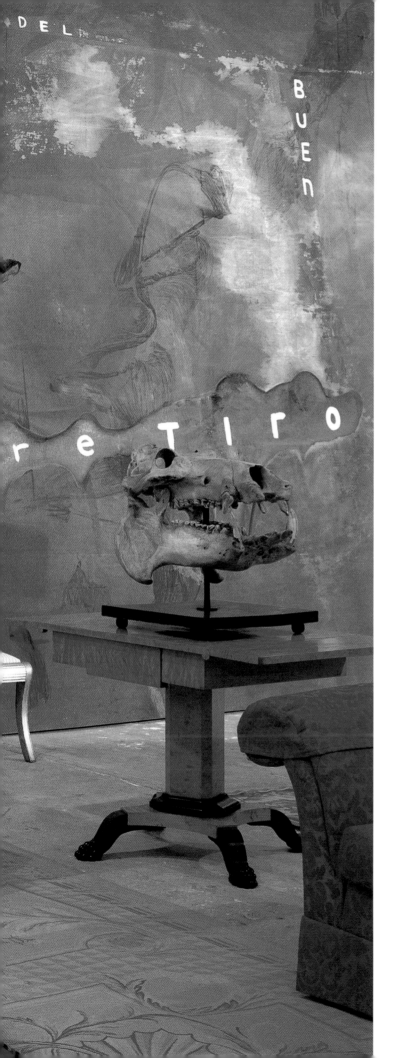

Operatic in scale and
design, this vast New York
loft on the second floor of
a nineteenth-century
perfume factory is home
to American artist Julian
Schnabel. Mixing austere
cement walls (above),
extravagant furniture and
his own giant, richly
coloured paintings (left),
he has given the interior
the feel of an ancient
Renaissance building.

Left **Schnabel's vast loft is perfect for housing his larger-than-life paintings, which can be as big as 16 feet (5 metres) square.**

Centre left **All manner of found objects are incorporated into the loft interior and into his paintings, from old tiles to ancient textiles.**

Bottom left **Schnabel found the building's original doors buried underneath steel beams and installed them at the entrance to his living room.**

Opposite **'Someone once said to me: you can't ruin a ruin,' says Schnabel who, even in the children's room, made no concessions to conventional decoration.**

crossing the atlantic

Given such success in the USA, it was only a matter of time before the concept of loft-living came to Europe. It appeared first in fits and starts as young, enterprising people who had experienced the scene in New York tried it out at home. In 1970 sculptor Yves de la Tour D'Auverngne, for example, converted a key factory in the Boulevard St Germain area of Paris*; in Britain, meanwhile, architect Tony Goddard was creating the first London loft building by turning a derelict Victorian tea warehouse on the banks of the Thames into Oliver's Wharf – a development of 23 largely open-plan apartments which were equipped with nothing but the basics. 'It was the first building in London to be converted like this,' he explains, 'and we weren't sure what the response would be. We put a tiny advert in the personal column of *The Times* for potential buyers and we had thousands of responses.'

Although there was evidently a demand for this new unstructured kind of living space in Europe, however, lofts did not take off on a grand scale at this stage. In London and Paris, for example, during the 1970s and 1980s loft-living was something reserved for the eccentric, the creative and the rich – the ad-man with his Le Corbusier armchairs, perhaps, or the film director with his collection of recherché modern art. It was very much an individual thing, not a general movement.

There are several reasons for this. As in New York a decade or so earlier, urban planning authorities did not welcome attacks on their industrial building stock. The bureaucracy involved in getting planning permission for change of use, even for unused industrial buildings, put off many an enthusiastic would-be developer. Also, those who did brave the bureaucracy frequently got the thing wrong. In London's Docklands area, for example, developers eager to make a quick buck converted old warehouses into expensive one-bedroom apartments that went against the entire ethos of the loft and, consequently, failed.

Many converted nineteenth-century buildings offer living spaces with the kind of overblown proportions that it is rare to find elsewhere.

With big-name **architects** and leading **designers** at the architectural helm, London's **lofts** became as much a **celebration** of modern design as a testament to the **industrial** past.

the london movement

It was in London, in the early 1990s, that things began to change. Thanks to Margaret Thatcher and the financial boom and bust of the 1980s, there was a glut of unused light-industrial buildings all over the city and local authorities suddenly changed their tune. Keen to get any sort of money for these properties and also eager to regenerate areas that were becoming increasingly down-at-heel, they began to welcome developers with open arms. When, in 1994, VAT was abolished on loft developments, there was no stopping them.

George Kozlowski and the Kentish Property Group PLC had set the ball rolling with the conversion of an old Bryant & May match factory in Bow, in the East End of London (a project later taken over by another developer, London Buildings). Marketed as 'New York loft-living in London's East side', this offered the public finished apartments, equipped with the essentials, and although these were necessarily more refined than the New York originals, they did have the right ingredients. Kitchens were open-plan; there was double-height space at the front of the building and the bedrooms were on galleries at the back. The brochure made the connection even more clearly: 'Naturally the warehouse style is faithfully maintained throughout the development … A vast steel and glass atrium sets the scene, while corridors with exposed steel ducts confirm the building's industrial origins.'

The scheme was a great success and London Buildings went on to convert industrial buildings all over the city into loft spaces. What made these work where others (notably the Docklands' developments) had failed was partly a matter of timing, but it was also a matter of quality. One of a new breed of developer who seemed to care just as much about the product being created as the profits being reaped, this company chose its sites very carefully, converting only those buildings they felt were of architectural interest (such as the beautiful Art Deco building at the core of their Alaska scheme in Bermondsey, South London). They also made sure their developments came up to the mark by getting big-name architects involved.

With many of the leading designers of the day at the architectural helm, these well-conceived London loft developments became as much a celebration of modern design as a testament to the industrial past. The British public couldn't help but be

The interior of a mews house by minimalist John Pawson, whose clean and linear architecture did much to shape the interiors of the first London lofts.

tempted by this new type of living space. It was not, however, just the architecture that got them going. Like middle-class New Yorkers before them, style-conscious Londoners were being wooed by the loft lifestyle that came with it and, more particularly, by the marketing strategy of the other key London loft developer, Harry Handelsman.

It was Handelsman, an ex-property investor, who arguably made the first big strike on the British consciousness in 1992 with his development of lofts in Clerkenwell (at that time a neglected area on the edge of the City). Having bought an old Art Deco printworks, he converted it into 23 loft 'shells' (in other words, raw, unfinished units) which had all the edginess of their predecessors in New York. That Handelsman managed to sell every one with ease, despite the fact that the project was launched the day after the financial crash of Black Wednesday, is testament to his skill at communicating the concept of loft-living to the conservative British public. Realizing that it might be tricky – at the very least – to persuade people whose only experience was of conventional housing to buy these empty shell spaces, Handelsman, with the help of George Kozlowski, masterminded a brilliant publicity

Above **Pawson opened up the ground floor of the house to create one large living space, broken up only by a few pieces of geometric furniture.**

campaign which focused on the lifestyle rather than the property. He threw a giant party in the newly acquired building, used it as an exhibition space and produced the first of many graphic and gritty brochures that was all about image. Combining funky lowercase type with grainy and seductive black-and-white photographs of downtown London, it was – according to Handelsman – 'more like a Paul Smith catalogue than a normal property brochure', and it did the job brilliantly for him.

Since that Clerkenwell project, Handelsman and his company, Manhattan Loft Corporation, have created a further five loft developments in London, all as well-publicized and successful as the first (but, of course, increasingly pricey), and they have sold the loft lifestyle to thousands of Brits. That these and other well-conceived developments have done wonders turning run-down areas of London into society's hot spots (Clerkenwell, Bankside, King's Cross et al) has helped to inspire a string of provincial developers and to woo local authorities nationwide. The trend for loft-living has, consequently, spread all over Britain.

Right **The stainless steel kitchen was reduced to the absolute essentials.**

the loft today

From its very modest beginnings 50 years or so ago, at the end of the twentieth century the loft has become a commercial commodity. Developments are continually springing up all over the world, turning loft-living into a global phenomenon. In the USA the loft has spread from its birthplace in New York to most other major urban centres – Chicago, San Francisco, Los Angeles and Detroit, for example. Canada, too, is catching up. Once loft-living was established in the early 1990s in Vancouver's Gas Town, it was not long before cities such as Montreal, Toronto and Calgary were being peppered with chic copycat developments.

In Europe, the process has been more gradual. While Britain has been at the epicentre of development, with lofts moving swiftly from London to Leeds, Bradford, Manchester and beyond, in the rest of Europe, loft-living has been, until now, more of a peripheral thing. Although in Belgium, Germany and France, for example, design-conscious individuals have been at it for years, major loft developers have been discouraged from taking lofts into the mainstream on account of planning restrictions and also because an existing supply of good alternative modern housing (something that Britain has always lacked) has meant that the demand for this new kind of living space has not been so pressing. Things look set to change, however, and major developers are now moving into cities all over the continent. Manhattan Loft Corporation, for one, have started developing sites in Paris, Cologne and Berlin.

Why this American invention, as surely as Coca Cola and McDonald's*, has taken the world by storm is not easy to sum up in a sentence. The loft, it seems, was just in the right place at the right time. The artists forged its identity; the film-makers consolidated its image; the planners and politicians eased its progress; and city dwellers worldwide, ready for a new adaptable, informal kind of living space, which could be all things to all people, welcomed it with open arms. Little wonder, then, that the loft has grown gradually, surreptitiously and organically from a marginal, bohemian retreat into the aspirational home of the millennium.

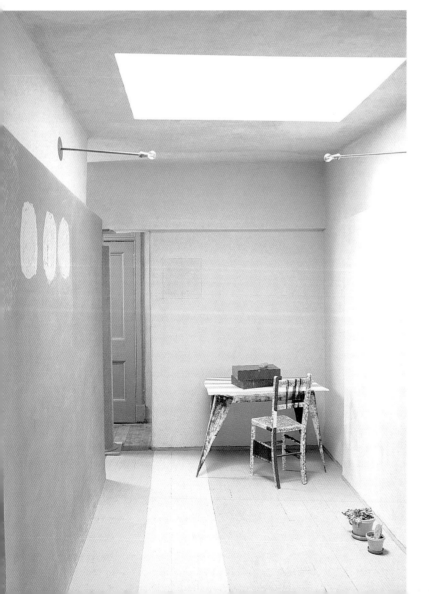

Left **With a wash of pale colour and understated decoration, this converted tenement apartment in Glasgow was turned into a calm, contemporary home.**

Opposite **An enclosed corridor in the middle of the interior was opened up on both sides to allow the sunlight to flow freely right through the space.**

2

the spaces

the outsides the insides

It is not only the vast **dimensions** and quality of **light** that appeal, it is also the feeling that **imbedded** in the **bricks** and **steel** of each old industrial building is the **story** of what went on inside it.

the outsides

industrial appeal

Lofts first carved a home for themselves in such old industrial buildings as flour mills, printworks, tea warehouses and hat factories. Their appeal to the early loft dwellers and, later, the developers is obvious: overscaled dimensions and symmetrical structures make perfect raw materials for conversion. But why have the rest of us gone along with them so eagerly? What is it about these very undomestic edifices that excites us?

Of course, many of them are beautiful to look at with their red bricks, giant windows or Art Deco facades, but there is more to their appeal than simple aesthetics. What attracts us, it seems, is a sense of their history as workplaces; the feeling that imbedded in the bricks and steel of each old industrial building is the story of what went on inside it. Steve Bowkett and Jane Tankard, two designers who

Many people have been drawn to lofts by the beautiful facades of the ex-industrial and commercial buildings in which they are often located and, as a result, many previously run-down areas of cities like New York have become stylish and sought-after enclaves of modern urban living.

converted an old nineteenth-century warehouse in London, reveal the appeal of such spaces when, describing their own, they talk of the 'fragments of materials and memories retained by every surface … the floor scarred from generations of seamstresses' shoes that had pitted the soft orange timbers'.

It is a romantic notion, naturally; a rose-tinted hankering after a nobler, better time, when machines whirred, children ran errands and people had parties in the street, but this celebration of our industrial past is not pure nostalgia. It is tied up with that modernist idea of function being more important than form and it is also encouraged by our desire to preserve an industrial heritage which, in cities worldwide, is being systematically pulled down. By living in a loft we can, of course, have the best of both worlds: we can honour the past but at the same time be absolutely modern.

With their huge expanses of window, the interiors of these ex-industrial or commercial buildings have an unsurpassed quality and quantity of light.

from warehouse to work space

Although at first lofts were defined by the very fact that they were carved out of old industrial buildings, this definition has had to be broadened precisely because there is a limited supply of old and attractive warehouses still standing. Developers – resourceful to the last – have had to look elsewhere for potential loft buildings and, consequently, we have seen a new wave of conversions in other areas. First, old public institutions became the targets: nineteenth-century schools, libraries and even churches. These shared the overblown proportions and, often, the symmetrical structure of old warehouses and factories (a useful quality for developers for whom regular windows, for example, are key when it comes to slicing up a building into roughly equal-sized living spaces).

More recently, eager-eyed developers have turned their attention to more contemporary commercial properties – office blocks from the 1960s, 1970s and 1980s, for example – and have even started to construct their own purpose-built 'loft buildings'. Although these necessarily come without some of the original loft accoutrements (freight lifts, heavy iron doors, the patina of the working past), the best follow the industrial prototype and offer living spaces with giant windows, high ceilings, vast floor areas and, of course, flexibility.

In many ways some of these new lofts better the originals, or at least offer contemporary benefits that old buildings cannot. At The Glass Building, a recently completed loft development in London by Piers Gough of the architectural practice CZWG, the entire facade (as the name suggests) is window. As Gough comments: 'The design of the building is based on qualities often found in loft-conversion schemes. Qualities of light, space and materials. But here, because the building is new, with added advantages in quality, practicability and amenity.'

Old industrial or commercial buildings are, however, still the jewel in the crown of loft development and because today it is more common to find these buildings in isolation, sandwiched between other, less rarefied properties, many developers have started to create loft schemes that mix old buildings with new. Bankside, Harry Handelsman's flagship development in London where he himself lives, comprises, for example, a Victorian warehouse, a 1960s office block and the newly built Millennium Tower. Similarly, many loft developments that have recently been completed in the USA, Canada, Australia and the rest of Europe often start with the conversion of an old industrial building and then expand into something new.

open space and light are

the locations

Loft buildings today are clearly a diverse bunch but what they generally have in common is location. Whether you are looking in Vancouver or Leeds, you will find that lofts congregate in the same kind of urban areas: on the banks of rivers; alongside railway lines; in run-down and derelict city districts; anywhere, in fact, where there is a glut of old, disused warehouses, factories or office blocks ripe for conversion.

These locations are not, of course, instantly attractive. They are down-at-heel and shabby. They lack, at least in the early days of the development, the amenities that are found in most residential areas. They feel, to many potential loft dwellers, unfamiliar and threatening. Indeed, for devotees, that is half their appeal; the rawer the area, it seems, the better. As journalist Peter Silverton noted, 'All loft dwellers are pioneers of a sort, conquering seemingly hostile inner-city areas.'

But, pioneering spirit aside, there are more practical benefits to living in these very urban locations. For anyone working in the city centre, for a start, the bonuses are obvious. Your office is on your doorstep, so you can stay in bed longer and get home earlier, and – if you are lucky – you may be able to walk to work. For those who aren't working, too, there are enormous benefits: being so

centrally located you are close to shops, cinemas, theatres and restaurants; you are part of the buzz of the city, which never fails to attract. As David Puttnam explains, 'The very idea of someone leaving the centre of [a city] to seek fame and fortune in a garden suburb just doesn't work, does it? – and it's hard to believe it ever will. From the earliest recognizable urban communities of 5,000 years ago, cities have been the driving force of human affairs – and they remain the irresistible destination of all those who insist on being where things are happening.'*

The majority of loft spaces are found in urban areas, but there are some striking exceptions. One such example is this old water tower, which is set in a wooded copse on the outskirts of Antwerp. This unusual building has been converted into a sleek, quirky and covetable contemporary home by its owner Jan Moereels and architect Jo Crepain.

what make a loft a loft

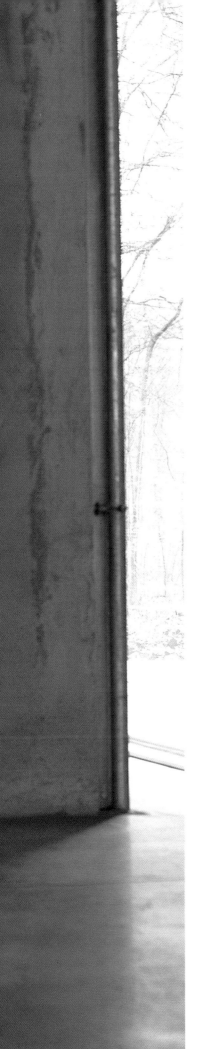

What is more, after the arrival of a loft building (if developers are to be believed) an area doesn't stay run down for long. Bringing with it an influx of people with money and aspirations, a well-conceived development will soon attract new businesses and amenities. Harry Handelsman, with his admirable track record of turning around the fortunes of several rough areas, is understandably confident: 'If Manhattan Loft Corporation get involved in a certain area, their reputation would in itself validate and help to regenerate that area,' he claims. And many loft developments – particularly those which are situated in less central locations – have started to bring the amenities with them. Increasingly there are schemes that incorporate cafés, gym facilities and even shops into the development, creating, in essence, a microcosm of the city.

So, it is not difficult to see why governments worldwide have been so receptive to the loft phenomenon. It seems to have everything going for it. It is creating new urban living spaces out of old, disused properties and saving the countryside from overdevelopment by salvaging derelict buildings on brownfield sites. It is celebrating the industrial past while at the same time forging an identity for the future. And, most crucially of all, by attracting money and creativity, it is transforming depressed inner-city, non-residential areas into desirable urban enclaves of contemporary living.

The base of the water tower is a simple concrete box punched with giant windows. On the ground floor is a minimal living room with staggering views across the park and a pared-down kitchen with worktop and dining table combined, allowing Moereels to chat with his friends as he cooks.

the insides

It used to be easy to define a loft. It was an entire floor of an old industrial building. It had giant windows and high ceilings. It had vestiges of its blue-collared past in the details: a freight lift, perhaps; a concrete floor or metal doors with heavy iron hinges. As the phenomenon has grown, however, lofts have appeared which do not quite match this description in buildings that could hardly be described as industrial. The term 'loft', it seems, can now encompass slices of 1960s and 1970s office blocks; bits of old educational buildings; even apartments in newly built developments.

For those purists who worry about authenticity, this has become an issue. New purpose-built developments, for example, are not strictly lofts in the true sense of the word, but does it really matter? The original – a giant swathe of industrial space – is obviously the ideal and what every loft since has been trying to emulate, but the newer loft apartments in old public buildings or newer commercial ones can be just as valid, as long as they share the loft ethos, if not the essence.

Loft-living is about a state of mind; about a love of light and space and the city – and as long as you feel your loft is up to the mark, don't worry about its pedigree. As Tyler Brûlé, editor of design magazine *Wallpaper*, says: 'Behind closed doors you can pursue a Warholesque notion of living in your own factory. So much of our culture is, after all, about playing out lifestyle fantasies.'* However, it is important to realize that not all spaces sold as 'lofts' even come close to the real thing, so to avoid getting sold short, make sure your loft fulfils the following 'lofty' criteria.

**Once used by *Vogue*
for storing patterns, this
London warehouse (right)
is now home to many
sleek modern lofts which,
thanks to the overscaled
windows, are flooded
with sunlight (above).**

what makes a loft a loft?

space

An absolute must. Even if a loft is not in an industrial building, it should seem industrial in scale. Ceilings should be high – between 10 feet (3 metres) and 14 feet (4.25 metres), compared to a 7-foot (2-metre) average in other residential buildings – and the floor area as vast as possible. Some of the best lofts are the biggest. Katleen Van Zandtweghe has a mammoth juice factory in Belgium, which covers 12,912 square feet (1,200 square metres); Yumi Matote has 5,000 square feet (465 square metres) of space in an old flour warehouse on the banks of the Thames.

But spacious doesn't have to mean big. Some of the newer developments offer mini lofts (targeted at younger, less affluent buyers), which have a sense of space although they are just 700-800 square feet (65-74 square metres) in size; the equivalent of a conventional one-bedroom conversion. The key to creating that spacious feel is to divide up your loft as little as possible; an open interior will automatically seem bigger.

light

The other key loft ingredient and the thing that sold New York's artists the lifestyle in the first place. Before you buy a loft, make sure there is a good ratio of window to wall so that light can pour into the interior. Also, if you are not occupying an entire floor of a building, think about how to bring daylight to the more remote spaces at the back of the loft (skylights are possible if you are on the top floor and daylight bulbs can do wonders).

Architect Vincent Van
Duysen has maximized
the light in his Belgian
loft by using bleached
wood on floors and
shelves, and also by
eliminating clutter.

openness

A loft must be at least partly open-plan, with as few conventional walls as possible (that is the whole point, after all). Those who want to be the most authentic go the whole hog and do without rooms altogether (although a separate bathroom is an accepted concession even for purists). Some keep their living space and kitchen open but create private bedrooms at the back. If you are buying the loft as a shell, you can, of course, decide exactly how to divide up your space – or not (see space planning, page 58); if you are buying a fitted-out loft (one that has been equipped by the developer with the basics like bathroom and kitchen units) you will have to make do with what you are given – although generally these, too, will be left as open-plan as possible.

urban landscape

A tricky one this because it is not absolutely essential and there are some great loft-style buildings on the outskirts of cities and even in the country. But, it must be said, views of trains, planes and automobiles all add to the – dare I say it – loft experience.

industrial elements

Again not crucial, but Duncan Chapman of Circus Architects is not alone when he defines the loft as: 'A fitted-out shell where the reverberations of the industrial past can still be felt.' So, for that genuine look, the more exposed pipes and bare bricks the better, and if your loft hasn't got industrial kudos in the structure, add it in the details (see the industrial look, page 154).

By using a mixture of tactile materials, Van Duysen has turned this ex-office space into a pared-down but very sensual interior.

the interiors

While space, light and industrial details are what make a loft, what you do with them is your own business. There is no one prototype to follow these days and no one typical loft. As Paola Gallo explains in her book *Lofts in Italy*: 'Although from a typological point of view the features of loft design are relatively specific what makes them an exceptional and manifold laboratory in which to try out lifestyles and alternatives to the traditional modes of living is the substantial absence of layout constrictions and the consequent privilege of being able to arrange the domestic or working environment around criteria that are wholly individual.'

So, although the loft is seen as a single category within the housing arena, it is the most diverse of living spaces, which today incorporates everything from split-level penthouses to open-plan apartments; refined slices of old commercial property to rough and ready sweeps of industrial space. And the way you choose to decorate your own loft is entirely up to you (see chapter four for ideas). It can be glamorous, comfortable or full of factory fittings. It can be modern or classical. It can be all things to all people. The loft is, when it comes down to it, the ultimate democratic space that can make anyone, whatever their taste or inclination, feel in tune with the times.

Architect Gaap Dakman turned this vast old church in the centre of Amsterdam into a giant living-cum-work space with a mezzanine floor and a wall of windows.

3

design directions

is loft-living for you?
doing your own conversion
buying a shell buying off-
the-shelf **before-you-buy
tips** renting a loft

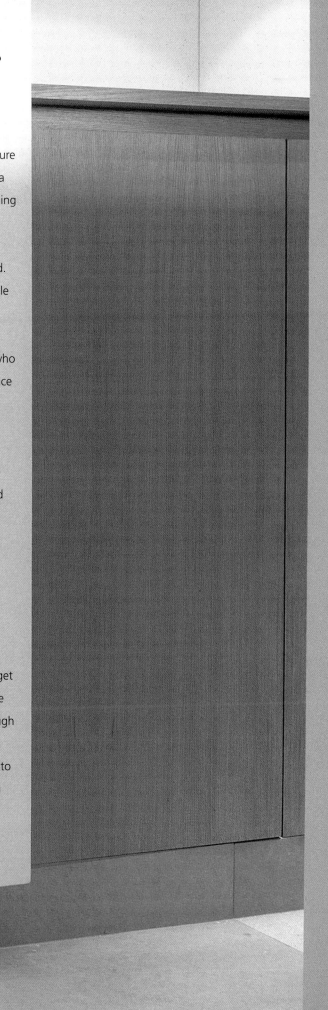

is loft-living for you?

Buying a house is always a tricky business, but usually you know what you are getting – two bedrooms, a dishwasher, the odd historical feature – and you know how much it will cost. Buying a loft – particularly in shell form – is a different thing altogether. What you get for your money is an empty box and simply the potential to create exactly the living space you have always wanted.

It is not surprising, then, that so many people are seduced by the concept, only to find that putting it into practice proves to be more complicated than they had anticipated. Many who buy into the idea of loft-living have no experience of renovating a home beyond a bit of painting, and tackling the business from scratch can be daunting at the very least. What is more, with a loft, there is so much to think about from the word go. Is it best to buy a ready-made loft and just move in? Is it more satisfying to get a shell and design it yourself? Most important of all, how much will it cost? Although the thought of creating a unique, personalized living space appeals to the artist in all of us, it is easy to be scared off by the scale of such a challenge.

The best thing to do is to look at lots of different lofts to see which ones you like best; get advice from the professionals and talk to people who have gone through the experience. Although there are many options to choose from (see below), with a little research it is relatively easy to work out which would be best for you. Moving into a loft will take time, effort and inevitably more money than you anticipate but, for what you get in exchange, it is well worth it.

doing your own conversion

You can picture the scene: a lovely old, empty warehouse on the edge of the city; the allure of authentic loft-living; the challenge of doing it all yourself. Who wouldn't be tempted?

But before you put your house on the market and start trawling salvage yards for industrial-style furnishings, do your homework and consider carefully whether you – and your finances – are up to the task. This is the bravest option of all and one only for the dedicated. Here is a checklist of some of the things you will need to think about before you begin:

- If you find a great building, keep quiet about it. If a developer or other potential buyers hear about it, they might beat you to it.
- If you are thinking of buying and converting a place with others, choose a building with regular windows so you can develop a series of naturally lit rooms inside. Also, make sure there are enough blank panels to allow space for partition walls.
- Getting planning permission for change of use is crucial (if you don't get it you may find yourself being charged commercial rates for the property) but obtaining it can be a lengthy process and appraisers may only give residential status once the building has been converted.
- Generally you will have to put down a lump sum to convince a mortgage lender that you are committed to the property, and you must also be able to show evidence of a regular income.
- The building must be sound – a structural survey is essential.
- You will need to cost out the conversion carefully before you commit yourself.
- The interior should adhere to standard residential building regulations. You will need to find out exactly what these are.
- Make sure all services are provided for – power, gas, water and waste pipes, and also background ventilation, opening windows and locations for flues, etc. (these will need to be approved by the local authorities).
- Collective conversions make most sense. Not only will you be able to share the responsibility of the project with someone, you will also be able to buy materials in bulk and, therefore, at a lower price. If you can buy collectively, try to include someone with relevant experience in the group – a professional architect, builder, surveyor or lawyer.

Despite this cautionary list, don't be put off converting a building yourself if you think you can do it. It will mean you get exactly what you want where you want it and it can save you money. Steve Bowkett and Jane Tankard, who in 1995 together with seven others bought a warehouse in Nile Street, London, got more than 2,000 square feet (186 square metres) of space for just £36,000 ($57,600), with development and services costing an extra £20,000 ($32,000). In Manhattan Loft Corporation's subsequent Nile Street development, a shell of that kind of size would have cost you around £400,000 ($640,000).

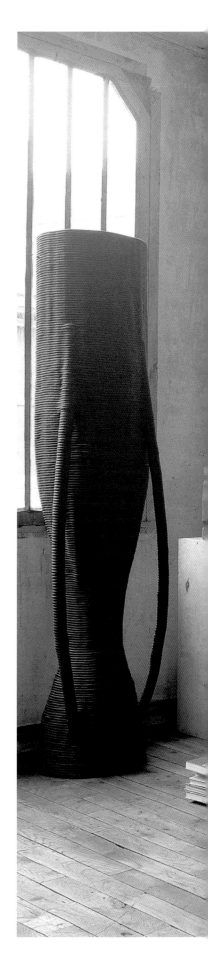

Fashion designer Jean Colonna did the bare minimum to his loft in an old Parisian shoe factory, adding only simple concrete structures to divide up the space.

buying a shell

Buying an unfinished loft is the ultimate opportunity for self-expression because, unlike any other residential property on the market, you can design the entire space yourself from scratch. Where else would you have the freedom to choose where to put the walls, what kind of floor to have, how big your bedroom should be? All very inspiring of course, but beware: whether you decide to design the shell yourself or commission someone else to do it for you, consider the project very thoroughly before you begin. Planning a home is a mammoth operation and it is crucial to be aware of exactly what you are taking on right from the start. Even before you buy, think about the following:

location, location, location

The mantra of the estate agents, location is something we have traditionally held in high esteem when it comes to home-buying but, arguably, it is less important for loft dwellers than anyone else. Loft developments tend to be sited in the less appealing areas of the city; in the haunts of old industrial buildings or simply somewhere the developer could buy cheaply. Don't be put off by this. The likelihood is that the lofts themselves will start to turn the area around, that debris and graffiti will soon give way to shops, restaurants and bars (see pages 35–6). Keep in mind, however, that the professionals' advice is to buy the best shell you can in the best development you can afford (from the point of view of resale if nothing else). And, one note of caution: make sure there are no vast shopping malls, parking areas or further developments about to be built next to yours, or the views of the urban cityscape

that sold you the place might turn out to be a little less panoramic than you remember.

the site

Whatever loft building you choose, make sure it is being converted by a developer with a successful track record and that there is a good architect on board. Even if you decide to do the work on your shell yourself, it is important that the communal areas – the entrance, the lifts – are well designed, both for your own benefit and to add value to your loft. Also, find out if there is to be further building on your site. If, for example, there are plans for a penthouse to be constructed on the roof, be prepared to put up with months of dust and noise and negotiate compensation.

the budget

Be realistic. Buying, designing and furnishing a loft always costs more than you think. For a start, it is very hard to get a 100 percent mortgage for a shell (and some lenders refuse even 80 percent), so you will have to put down a lump sum at the beginning. Then you will have to pay for somewhere to live while your loft is being made habitable (a period of between five and eight months is average). Finally, there is the cost of the work itself (see below), for which you should budget at least £50/$80 per square foot (£500/ $800 per square metre) and, additionally, the fees of any architect or interior designer you commission to help.

Buying a loft shell and building an interior from scratch gives you absolute decorative freedom and structural flexibility.

a) the DIY fit-out

Once you have bought your shell it is easy to get carried away by thoughts of glamorous suede sofas and stainless steel lights, but decorating a loft is not just about the cosmetics. It is about building the bones of a home to make it just right for you, so you must get the structure sorted out before you start thinking about the finishing touches. What needs to be dealt with first is the nitty gritty – the heating, the plumbing, the sound-proofing (things that are particularly important in a loft with its big windows and high ceilings) – and the layout of the space. Once you have got this right, you can indulge your furnishing dreams in comfort.

the builders

You can't begin without builders, so make sure you find good ones. Get recommendations from friends or colleagues and interview several before you make your selection. If you want to project-manage the building work yourself, you will be able to save around 30 percent on the cost of the work on your loft (see cost, page 73), but going down this route can be risky and fraught with problems. You will need to co-ordinate the various comings and goings of the plumber, the electrician, the carpenter, the painter, etc. and brief them very precisely. You will also need to make sure they work together on the project rather than independently to avoid mishaps (new electricity outlets being painted over or cables being sawn in half, for example) and this can be a complicated, time-consuming and frustrating task, particularly if the workmen do not communicate effectively with each other or with you and 'pass the buck' when a problem does arise. To avoid the hassle and inevitable stress of doing the job yourself, you may choose to employ a contractor to manage the building work for you. If you do, although you will not save much money on the work costs, you should save your sanity.

the nitty gritty

A shell, just as the word suggests, is essentially an empty space. If you are converting the building yourself, you will be lucky to get a space that already has workable walls, floors and ceilings. If, on the other hand, you are buying into a development, these should have been cleaned and made good. If the existing structure is of poor quality, think about creating 'floating' walls (essentially a shell within a shell), which will give you a smooth finish but also keep the existing architecture intact should you have a change of heart and want bare bricks back again. (Incidentally, leaving a small space at the tops, bottoms and sides of such walls blurs the perimeters of the loft and will make it seem bigger.

Developers generally offer what they call a 'serviced shell', which means that entrance doors have been fitted and all the standard services (water, electricity, phone cables, etc.) brought up to the loft and capped off. Read the small print of developers' brochures carefully to find out exactly what is included. Some create two service points in each shell to give more flexibility when it comes to positioning the kitchen and bathroom.

Several loft buildings also come with a centralized heating system, but this can have its disadvantages. The Alaska loft scheme in South London was nicknamed Baked Alaska when – in the early stages – the system went wrong and kept all the lofts at enormously high temperatures. If you are sorting out the heating yourself, remember that you are not dealing with a conventional house. Choose something suitable for the space and consider unusual methods, such as underfloor heating, which can work brilliantly in a loft and eliminate the need for radiators.

As a response to the unconventional needs of loft dwellers, manufacturers are constantly coming up with new problem-solving products, so do your research carefully before you start and keep up to date. One of the latest innovations is Priva-Lite: an insulating material that can be sandwiched between two panes of glass to prevent your loft from overheating in summer and freezing in winter. Translucent when an electric current is passed through it but opaque when the current is switched off, Priva-Lite is also good for screening the interior from view. Another useful innovation is Folia – a substance which, when used to cover your windows, will blur the view of people looking in from the outside and also take 90 percent of the heat and bleaching powers out of the sun. Don't forget, however, that new technology of any kind will not come cheap.

When you are planning how to divide up your interior, try to keep it as open-plan as you can to maximize the feeling of space and light. The owners of this London loft let the sitting room (left and above) and the kitchen (below) flow freely into one another, creating one enormous living space that is both functional and comfortable. Also, by using the same palette of hot and funky colours in each area, they made sure that the two work well together.

space planning

This is the most crucial and also the most difficult thing to get right. While it is amazingly empowering being able to dictate exactly what your home should look like – to choose where you will work, where you will play and how big your bathroom will be – it is also easy to be bewildered and daunted by the freedom of it. How many bedrooms do you really want? Where should they go? Should you divide up your space or leave it entirely open?

Some of these decisions will be made for you by building regulations (which are the same for any residential property). Even your quota of 'habitable rooms' will have been set by the developer and the planners (you can't exceed this without getting new consent, so make sure you know what the figure is). But even once you have heeded the rules, you will still have a huge amount of flexible space to play with.

Consider various alternatives. Write lists of what you need (room to hang 50 suits, a home office, a big kitchen or whatever), draw sketches of the different permutations your space could take and decide on a scheme that will maximize the bonuses of your particular loft and minimize its faults. Most importantly, keep in mind that you bought the place precisely because it offered unadulterated space and light, so do your best to retain that lofty essence. If you have got ceilings twice the height of those in a conventional house, shout about it.

Although at first sight, it might seem easiest – and most authentic – to leave your loft entirely open-plan, consider whether this would really work for you. Are you as free and easy as you think? And if you are, what about your guests? Where would you put your mother-in-law if she came to stay? And would you be able to relax if you could see dirty dishes from your bedroom?

An open-plan layout, with all its free-flowing, adaptable space, suits some people down to the ground. Devotees eulogize about being able to cycle around the furniture (never mind the skid marks), chat while they bathe and entertain 100 people in the living 'room'. These are not qualities to be sniffed at, of course, and the biggest fans – perhaps surprisingly – are those who have the largest lofts; as though having a giant floor area makes division even more difficult.

For others, however, completely open-plan living is not ideal. Designer Peter Wylly, for example, who works and lives in his London loft found that he had to create a physical barrier between his living area and his working area to stop him thinking about one thing when he was doing the other (see pages 80–1).

By creating one multi-purpose space for cooking, eating and entertaining, the owner ensured she could chat with her friends as she worked.

If you do decide to divide up your loft, don't feel you have failed. It is not a compromise if it is done cleverly and does not detract from the space itself. Also, on the positive side, it enables you to introduce a variety of structures and forms that will add architectural interest to what can otherwise be an unremittingly rectilinear space. Even lowering the ceilings or raising the floor in sections of your loft can be beneficial. Although it might seem anathema to intrude on the raw space in this way, a differentiation of height can, paradoxically, make the place feel more spacious.

Think, too, of unexpected ways to split one part of the loft from another. Use curved partitions, for example (also good for softening the hard lines of most lofts) or, like Philip Billingham and Heidi Wish (see page 16), create a central barrier to separate the private areas from communal. And consider the materials carefully. They chose to use red laminated glass in their loft space, which not only created a funky, alternative screen but also, importantly, let the light through.

Think of ways to divide up your interior without enclosing it. These graphic floor-to-ceiling doorways, for example, separate one area from another but let the light through.

Another dividing device that has been greatly exploited in lofts all around the world is the mezzanine. Like a glorified gallery, this splits a section of the loft horizontally, allowing you to keep double-height space in one area (making the most of those high ceilings), while creating private 'rooms' underneath the platform in another; or, as architect Duncan Chapman more properly explains, it gives you 'scope for spatial exploration in section'. Mezzanines are brilliant for bed decks, work spaces or even living areas (and they give you the additional bonus of making a feature out of a staircase) but there is one catch: they are only a possibility if the floor-to-ceiling height is at least 12 feet (3.7 metres) because there should be a minimum of 4½ feet (1.4 metres) above the platform to allow comfortable movement, such as sitting up in bed, for example.

Previous page **By splitting this giant loft in two with a mezzanine, the architect created rooms at the back while retaining the double-height space at the front.**

Opposite **Mezzanines are supremely versatile space-dividers. They can make great bed decks, as here, work spaces and even high-rise living areas.**

Above **A mezzanine will also allow you to make a feature of the stairs, as in this London loft where the sculptural spine-like stair-case steals the show.**

This page **Wanting to partition her vast, converted warehouse as little as possible, Els Lybeert came up with ingenious ways of dividing one area from another. A large oblong 'box' (left), which runs all the way along one side of the space, accommodates the kitchen, cloakroom and stairs up to the bedrooms on the mezzanine floor (right and below).**

Next page **A frosted-glass sliding door allows Lybeert to leave the kitchen open or hide it from view.**

When it comes to deciding which 'rooms' should go where, think about how you use your space. Designing a loft is all about creating somewhere that is just right for you, so analyse your lifestyle and create a layout to suit it. If you spend most of your time working at home, for example, put your office in the prime location; if you have always dreamt of having an enormous bedroom, give yourself one and adapt the rest of the space accordingly. It is also crucial to think about how natural light enters the building so that you do not place the most important areas in the darkest spaces.

While a little bit of division is understandable, don't be tempted to slice up your loft too much. The best thing about having creative freedom when it comes to planning your space is that you can do away with the traditional notion of having one room for each function. Who, these days, really wants the constraints of having a separate kitchen, dining room and living room? Inspired by the informal lifestyles portrayed in style magazines, what we crave instead is the flexibility provided by one big space where we can cook, eat, lounge, relax and entertain – and the loft cries out for us to create it. Rather than compartmentalizing your space with fixed walls and partitions, try to create multipurpose areas or divide your loft simply into practical living zones and private comfort zones.

the key to the best

The key to the best loft layouts is convertibility – being able to alter your space according to your mood – and, as journalist Jane Withers noted, 'the secret of the transformable apartment lies in the dexterity of the planning'. So think carefully about how to format your interior so that it will adapt itself to your changing needs. A foldaway wall, for example, or some sliding doors can give you privacy when you want it and openness when you don't. A built-in pull-down bed can make an instant bedroom out of what, at other times, is an office area (for more on doubling up space, see page 130). It is important to think about these kind of details right at the start, so you can incorporate them into the structure of your loft and gain bags of flexibility for the future.

The other thing you must consider at the planning stage is storage. It might sound dull, but it is the key to successful modern life. Lofts are about unfettered space, sweeps of uninterrupted floor and as little clutter as possible, so the more storage you build into the structure the better (particularly as you will not pay tax on any building work you carry out if it is an original conversion and not a ready-developed space).

lofts is convertibility

There are countless ways of incorporating inspired storage solutions into your loft, so think about what would be best for you – hidden cupboards, built-in shelves or box units, for example (see page 146 for more ideas). In a converted library in South London, Granit Architects came up with an ingenious storage solution for their clients: an entire wall of boxes and cupboards (see page 64), which accommodates the boiler, the television, the music system and all kinds of clutter. In addition to the practicality of the design, painted here and there in brilliant primary colours, it looks visually striking and becomes a feature in its own right. Incorporating your storage into the fabric of the loft itself is a clever trick which, by reducing the amount of freestanding furniture you will need to buy, also maximizes the potential for lots of unadulterated space.

Built-in furniture (above) and hidden storage (right) make it far easier to keep an interior clutter-free.

materials

Lofts, with their industrial heritage, have brought an array of new materials to the domestic environment – steel, aluminium, glass, concrete, rubber. A generation ago these would only have been seen in factories or functional Modernist buildings but are now cropping up in most stylish living spaces. It is all to do with that industrial aesthetic, and in a loft it works particularly well. Ex-factory spaces are suited to ex-factory fabrics, materials which are practical, durable and generally (though not always) cheaper than their more refined domestic counterparts.

But just because you live in a loft it doesn't mean you have to follow the industrial formula. If you are after a softer modern look, use less hard-edged materials: choose grainy wood, smooth stone or even carpet for floors; and cover those bare bricks with a textured plaster finish. If you want something novel, unearth unexpected, innovative materials, such as recycled plastic or laminated glass for an interior wall. These days, anything goes. Just make sure you choose materials that match your budget. (For more ideas, see chapter four).

cost

How much you spend on fitting out your loft is – to a point – up to you. To save money you can project-manage the work yourself (see page 54) or you can choose to use inexpensive materials. Covering a floor in plywood, for example, will cost considerably less than doing it in hardwood; fitting a stainless steel kitchen will set you back much more than one made from MDF. The important thing is to get the balance right and be creative.

Some of the cheapest materials can make the most impact if they are cleverly used and by economizing in one place, you might be able to splurge somewhere else. As Australian-based architect Tina Engelen commented: 'Budgeting a building project is like building up one's wardrobe of clothes. You buy an expensive Prada jacket – which gives you the overall look – and wear Gap T-shirts and generic pants underneath.'* As a rough guide, expect to pay at least £50/$80 per square foot (£500/$800 per square metre) for the work – £70/$112 (£700/$1,120) plus is more likely – and 30 percent less if you don't use a contractor. To avoid nasty financial surprises at the end, set yourself a budget and stick to it.

The other thing to keep in mind when you are spending lots of hard-earned cash designing your loft is whether you will get your money back when you to sell it. As a general rule, if the building is in good condition as far as structure and services are concerned and it is in a reasonable location, you should; although everything from the quality of the surrounding landscape to the parking facilities can make a difference.

b) Commissioning an architect

why an architect?

Manhattan Loft Corporation's first piece of advice to customers buying a shell is to employ an architect. 'If you have invested hundreds of thousands of pounds buying the place, it is just not economical to get a builder to knock a few walls together,' they assert. While they might, of course, be underestimating the skill of many a DIY loft designer, they do have a point. Few of us have the time, the inclination or the expertise to undertake such a vast building project, and commissioning an architect, while it should save you months of effort and anguish, should not limit your creative scope at all but increase it.

For a start, whether you have bought a raw space or a converted loft from a developer, an architect will sort out all the nitty gritty for you: what services are supplied; how many rooms you can have; any rules and regulations you will need to adhere to (whether you will have to have a fire escape, for example). They will also find, brief and negotiate with the builders (although even an architect can't guarantee that this will be a completely smooth process).

Having someone to take charge of the boring bits will leave you free to think about the fun stuff: what colour your walls should be and what kind of rubber tiles you would like in the bathroom. But an architect offers you far more than simply practical support. Coming up with creative solutions to any problems you have as far as your living space is concerned is the integral part of the architect's job, and they should be able to bombard you with countless inspiring possibilities for your home.

Architect Gunnar Orefelt was asked to turn this old sorting office (right) into a home and artist's studio. Rather than create a mezzanine at the back of the interior and keep the double-height space at the front, he did the reverse, so you emerge from a semi-enclosed hall between two giant 'boxes' containing the bedrooms, bathrooms and library, into the open, sun-filled studio beyond (opposite).

how to make it work

If you do decide to commission an architect, make sure you choose the right one. You need to find someone who is professional, of course, but also someone whose ideas you like (ask to see pictures of their previous projects) and who you feel you can work with. The relationship between architect and client is necessarily a very close one and it is vital that you can communicate with each other from the word go. Shop around and interview several before you make a final choice.

Try to pick someone who has had experience designing lofts and who understands the particular nature of the building in which you have bought (if you are buying into a development, ask the developers for recommendations). On account of the explosion of lofts worldwide, many young architectural practices are becoming specialists in the field and it makes sense to tap into their knowledge of (and consequently solutions to) the particular problems of living in ex-industrial or commercial buildings.

Once you have got an architect on board, don't be tempted to take a back seat. He or she will be creating your home, after all, so be as involved as you can in the process. The fact that the loft-design business is becoming a profession in its own right brings with it a danger of lofts becoming formulaic, of architects developing a 'loft style', and the best way of making sure your space doesn't fall into that trap is by giving as much personal input into its design as you can.

Communication is key. Talk to your architect and tell him or her your ideas. Make it clear what you absolutely want to keep (the sense of space, the light, etc.) and what you don't mind losing. Tear pictures out of magazines or catalogues to give the architect an impression of the kind of look you are after. Talk about colours and materials, and choose the fittings together.

Most importantly, don't be daunted by their expertise. If they suggest something that you know you would not like, don't be afraid to say exactly what you think. While most architects work absolutely in the interests of their clients, there are some who have their own agenda and you might need to be fairly forceful to get your message across.

Be prepared, too, to get personal. As their aim is to design a space that is tailor-made for you, the architect will need to know quite a bit about your lifestyle. How many clothes have you got?

Are you tidy? Do you share your bath with anyone? Be honest – even if it is embarrassing – because that way you will end up with a living space that fulfils your every need.

cost

To avoid going bankrupt, make sure your architect knows your budget at the beginning and sticks to it – and don't forget to take their fees into consideration at the start. Basically, the more involved in the project an architect is, the more he or she will cost you. Most charge an hourly rate for their services or take a percentage of the total building costs (between 8 and 15 percent is the average) with more on top if you want project-management of the work on a day-to-day basis. Although employing an architect is an expensive business, it is a worthwhile one. What you should get for your money is a well-designed, custom-made space which – if you have chosen your architect wisely – will also prove to be a good investment.

Previous page and opposite
At the top of the space are the living, dining and cooking areas. The kitchen is a model of contemporary minimal design, with all the clutter hidden away inside a geometric yellow box of storage units.

c) Getting your loft Feng Shui'd

Feng Shui is the talk of the town these days, with countless rational people throwing out their iron beds, buying fish tanks and even moving house simply to adhere to its prescriptions. For at the core of this ancient Eastern art is the belief that if you harmonize the relationship between people and their environment, health, wealth and happiness will follow. Little wonder, then, that so many of us are at it, hoping that by changing our living spaces we will also be changing our fortunes.

Many of the directives are common sense and easy to follow (log fires are good, for example, because they encourage sociability; televisions should be shut away because they do not), but this art-cum-science is not just about the finishing touches. If you want to do the thing properly, the very position and structure of your home need to be assessed. Slanted walls and sloping ceilings, for example, can be detrimental to your health and your love life. So, where better to practise Feng Shui than in a loft shell where you are

plotting your home from scratch? If you are serious about following the principles, get a Feng Shui master to choose your loft with you to make sure you pick one in the most beneficial location. Take his advice about how the interior should be laid out and decorated (Feng Shui comes with a recommended paint palette), and then get an architect or builder to complete the job for you. Because Feng Shui calls for lots of light and uncluttered space, lofts have a lot going for them from the outset, but it also calls

for fresh air; something that is rare in the inner city. And you may well find that you need to install a fish tank (beneficial for your finances, apparently) to make sure you can pay for the conversion.

Designers Peter Wylly and Birgit Israel consulted a Feng Shui master to help them turn an ex-industrial shell into this tranquil, partially open-plan home that doubles up as a living and work space.

Left **In this spectacular riverside apartment, the architect cleverly balanced the cool glassy facade with a very warm and sensual interior.**

Above **The streamlined kitchen-cum-eating area follows the colour scheme of the rest of the space, with its mix of steel and honey-toned wood.**

Left **Simply furnished with a sleek oversized bed and built-in side tables, this bedroom is tranquil, muted and pared down. All of the clothes, shoes and clutter are accommodated in the adjacent dressing area, which has copious amounts of tailor-made storage.**

Below **Every room at the front of the apartment has views across the river.**

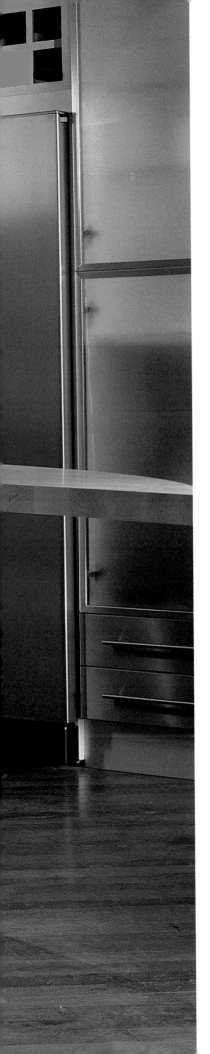

If you are **daunted** by the prospect of taking on a raw space, a **finished loft** could be the answer. Like '**pre-shrunk jeans**', developers 'structure the building to fit and then the **purchaser** steps into it'.

buying off-the-shelf

While there is a certain creative kudos about buying a loft shell and conceiving your own living space, don't let the image alone persuade you into it. Buying a shell is not the right option for everyone. Not for the first-time buyer, for example, who might find it hard to get a large enough mortgage (although lenders are becoming increasingly flexible). Not for the impatient, who want a new home right away. Not for the suspicious, who like to see just what they are getting for their money from the start. For these would-be loft dwellers, there is a far better alternative to go for: the ready-made loft.

Sometimes called a 'turn-key loft', this is a shell that has been designed by the developer and comes with all the basics supplied. What you will get for your money depends on which development you are buying into. As a general rule, you can expect to find a loft with a bathroom and kitchen already installed, and flooring and sometimes lighting included in the price. It

is 'a bit like pre-shrunk jeans', says architect Piers Gough. 'We structure the building to fit and then the purchaser steps into it' (a particularly apposite analogy given that jeans, like lofts, were transported from the workplace into the fashion world).

While it may cost you a little more than a cheap DIY equivalent (for a finished loft expect to add around 20 percent to the purchase price of a shell), this off-the-shelf approach to buying a loft has significant advantages. It offers you a new lifestyle in an instant (well, almost – unless, of course, you bought it at the planning stage and will have to wait for the work to be completed). It should be a relatively stress-free experience (no builders, plumbers or planners to worry about). And, because a developer will generally commission one architectural practice to do all the lofts in his building, you could get a loft designed by the next Richard Rogers much more cheaply than you would had you commissioned the same architect individually.

Developers will generally offer a fit-out service to anyone who wants it (read the brochure details carefully to make sure you understand exactly what the package comprises) and sometimes they will even develop a shell to your own specification. However, it tends to be the smaller-sized units that are sold ready-made

Part of a large-scale loft development in Leeds, this interior uses an effective combination of curves and colour to animate what was originally a smallish rectilinear space.

from the start. As Colin Serlin of developers London Buildings explains: 'In a huge unit there are so many different permutations the space can take that it makes sense to offer shells, to let people decide what to do with their own space, but if you have a smaller area of, say, 800 square feet (75 square metres), there is usually only one way it can be laid out, so it is more sensible for the developer to fit it out.'

Developed lofts are usually sold as standard, although there might be an element of choice included in the package (you may be able to choose between, say, a kitchen in stainless steel or wood). As such, they can obviously never offer the creative freedom of a shell but, if you buy into a good development, you should get all the lofty essentials (light, space, high ceilings) as well as an interior that is well designed and not overdone. Trying to appeal to a broad sweep of potential loft purchasers, developers and their architects try to keep things simple (plain floors, clean-lined kitchens, white walls, for example); to offer, in essence, the framework of a living space to which the buyer can then add his personal stamp.

And indeed, there is as much chance to be creative in this kind of space as in any conventional house. Just because the bare bones of the loft you buy may look like its neighbour does not mean the interior need follow the same formula. You can paint the walls; you can change the lights; you can fill the place with your own furniture. And if you haven't got the time, the energy or the inclination to do up the place yourself, consider commissioning an interior designer to do it for you.

A developer-finished loft need not mean a fussy, overdone interior. The decoration is usually kept to a minimum and the bare bones of a building left to speak for themselves.

employing an interior designer

The role of the interior designer has changed dramatically in the last 10–15 years. No longer someone who simply deals with the finishing touches of a living space – the curtains, the cushions, the colour of the walls – an interior designer today can offer you advice on things that have historically been the sole preserve of the architect. They can sort out the lighting and the heating, they can design you a kitchen, they can reconfigure the layout of your space. And nowhere is the overlap between architect and interior designer more evident than in a loft. Here, where traditional notions of heavy curtains and frilly furnishings have been abandoned, an interior designer will be as happy to advise you on sound-proofing your windows as an architect will be to find you the perfect stainless steel door handle.

So how do you choose which to use? If you are buying a shell (see page 53) it makes more sense, perhaps, to employ an architect who will have more expertise in the nitty gritty – the structure of a building, the building regulations, the service requirements, etc. (Although an interior designer can, of course, get architectural advice as and when they need it and, often, a provision for this will be included in their fee.) If you are buying a more developed loft, which needs little or no structural work but a good deal of creative input, it makes more sense to employ an interior designer.

Think about what you need and consider that the major difference between the two lies more in their approach to a project than in anything else. While the architect will tend to take the structure of your loft as a starting point and then work towards adapting it to your needs, the interior designer will tackle the job the other way around – they will consider how you want to treat the space first and then work out a way of channelling your

In this London loft, the interior designer has used dramatic sweeping curves to soften the hard edges of the otherwise angular space and also to define the different zones.

passions and tastes into a scheme that will work within the structure. If you are someone who likes to get excited about fabrics and furnishings right at the start, an interior designer is probably the best bet for you.

As with an architect (see page 74), choose who you commission carefully and make sure they know exactly the kind of look you are after. Think about the treatment that would best suit your lifestyle (low-maintenance, lots of storage space, washable upholstery or whatever) and get the designer to come up with a number of suitable possibilities (they will probably produce mood boards to give you an idea of what the final result might be). Do not be too conservative. Make the most of the fact that an interior designer will have insider knowledge of all the latest and best designs on the market and be willing to experiment with new products and materials.

Employing an interior designer can, if all goes smoothly, be a great short cut to creating an individual living space; a way to give your place a personal stamp without having to trawl the interior-design shops and scour the style magazines yourself. You will, of course, pay for the privilege, but what you end up with should be a loft with cutting-edge credentials and, more importantly, it should also be somewhere that functions perfectly for you and feels likes home. Just make sure you ask a few key questions before you commit yourself:

- How long will the project take?
- How much will it cost (interior designers usually charge around 8–12 percent of the project total)?
- Does the fee include day-to-day management of the project?
- Will you have to move out while the work is being completed? If you will, your costs will obviously increase.

Left top and bottom **Both the bedroom and bathroom in this loft are separated from the rest of the living space by a screen of sandblasted glass.**

Opposite **The original wooden floor was kept for the living area, but slate was laid in the dining 'room' to separate it visually from the main space.**

before-you-buy tips

- Vet the location in which you plan to buy to make sure it is somewhere you would feel happy coming home to. Think about noise from the street, parking (if it is not provided in your development) and public transport links.

- If you are buying a loft in a building that is still in the process of being developed, find out exactly what the construction plans are. If any new building work will affect you directly, negotiate compensation.

- Take into account that you will be living in a communal building and consider what this entails: potential noise from adjoining lofts (dividing 'stud' walls are not particularly thick); maintenance costs (these can be considerable if there are amenities, such as a gym, on site); the effectiveness of communal services (heating, water, gas or whatever).

- Find out at the start what kind of mortgage you can get. Historically banks or building societies would not give more than an 80 percent mortgage on the value of a shell, for example, so you had to stump up cash for the other 20 percent; some, however, are becoming increasingly flexible. Try to use a lender who has experience of lofts.

- Choose a solicitor who has had previous experience with lofts and don't rely on them to pick up the small print of disclaimers by developers. Read everything very carefully yourself and if you don't understand something, ask.

- Doing up a shell will cost more than you anticipate. Budget at least £50/$80 per square foot (£500/$800 per square metre) for equipping and decorating it, and be aware that you are more likely to spend £70/$112 (£700/$1,200) plus.

- Remember that you should not pay tax on the building work you carry out in your loft if it is an original, not a developed, conversion, so keep those receipts if you need to. Professional advice from an architect or interior designer, however, will be subject to tax.

- Don't underestimate the time it will take to get from raw space to finished product. The building work will inevitably take longer than you think.

- Lofts are sold with details of GIA (Gross Internal Area), but remember that this is not the same as usable floor space.

- Consider the drawbacks of living in a large, primarily open-plan, ex-industrial space. Big windows, for example, can mean substantial heat loss in winter and great heat gain in summer. Suitable insulation or air-conditioning will add to your costs considerably.

- If you are buying a developed loft, make sure all the windows are double-glazed and, ideally, fitted with draught excluders, to minimize both heat loss and noise.

- Scrutinize the specification of a developed loft carefully to make sure it is good quality and built to last. Also, note that

if interior party walls are built only to the minimum required by the building regulations, you may not be able to screw anything into them.

- Consider whether you will be able to get your furniture into the space without dismantling the windows. Has provision been made for easy access?
- If you are moving from a conventional house, your existing furniture may look out of place and out of scale in a loft. Add the cost of any extra furniture to your budget.
- Try renting a loft first to see if you like it.

An ingenious combination of freestanding boxes and moveable walls, this London loft by Mark Guard Architects is the ultimate transformable space.

renting a loft

It is all very well being seduced by the idea of loft-living but, as prices rise, not everyone can afford to buy a loft of their own. One solution – and a good way of testing whether the lifestyle is really the one for you – is to rent.

As the first generation of loft dwellers start to move on, there are increasingly more lofts-to-rent coming onto the market. Developers, too, are beginning to convert buildings specifically for rental, and many investors are buying lofts at the planning stage with a view to renting them out in the future. The rental sector, according to estate agents, is one that looks set to expand rapidly over the next few years.

These kinds of rented loft, however, don't come cheap. Individuals will be looking to recoup the money they spent on their own conversions and investors, naturally, seeking a healthy profit. If you choose to rent at this, the top end of the market, while you will not have to make the vast financial commitment you would if you were buying a loft, you will still see large chunks of money disappearing from your monthly salary.

By setting his kitchen in an oval structure right in the centre of his rented loft, designer Rock Galpin subtly and graphically divided his living area from his work space.

An S-shaped corrugated plastic screen creates a brilliantly fluid floor-to-ceiling partition between Galpin's studio and his presentation space.

A cheaper alternative is to approach the owner, landlord or developer of an unconverted building, who may be keen to rent out part of it on a short lease in return for a commitment from you to do a certain amount of work on it. Designer Rock Galpin fitted out a loft in a dilapidated curtain warehouse for a developer who was just beginning a conversion. The arrangement was mutually beneficial. Galpin got 2,500 square feet (232 square metres) of space for a small monthly rent, while the developer got a 'show apartment', which enabled him to sell the rest of the units.

This page **The freestanding oval kitchen is kept open to the main space with 'doors' at each end and eye-level slits that you can see and chat through.**

Opposite **The interior of the minimal kitchen is sleek and streamlined with the units, sink and worktop all finished in stainless steel.**

4

decoration
& design

choosing a scheme
dividing space choosing
your palette texture
multipurpose areas
flooring windows lighting
storage furniture the
industrial look the great
outdoors eating working
bathing sleeping

choosing a scheme

You've bought the loft, sorted out the heating, plumbing and insulation, and planned the layout of the space. What comes next is the most important part of all: deciding what your loft should look like. 'Be as creative with your space as you dare,' urges Manhattan Loft Corporation's promotional literature. 'You are in control. You can do whatever you want. You can have whatever you like...'

Yet having decorative carte blanche can be daunting. Now that fashion is targeting our homes as keenly as our wardrobes, we are spoilt for choice when it comes to deciding what flooring, fabric or furniture we should buy. And although the hard sell of the loft promoters is very persuasive, it is not strictly true. Overscaled, ex-industrial or commercial spaces come with their own decorative agenda and, to the make the most of your loft, you need to bear it in mind. Remember that you have got huge windows (frilly curtains are out), vast floors (designer carpet will cost you) and spaces

that flow freely into one another (no hiding those clashing colours behind closed doors).

What you need to do before you rush out and buy the latest designer must-haves is to come up with a scheme that you like and you can live with, but one that will also be cohesive and work well in your particular space. Think about the bare bones of your loft. They alone may dictate what should be done with it. Your space may be rigorously rectilinear and crying out for curvy furniture; it may be full of cool northern light and need a wash of warm colour; it may be – if you are lucky – full of industrial features and the ideal place to indulge your fantasy for factory fittings.

Think hard about what you want before you start. Be imaginative, be individual and do what feels right for you. A loft space can be all things to all people and if you decorate it in a way that maximizes the potential for flexibility, informality and creativity, you will end up with the ultimate personal, comfortable end-of-the-century home.

Creating an interior from scratch is the ultimate opportunity for self-expression. Italian designer Paola Navone chose to give her open-plan living area a global feel by filling it with an individual mix of furniture and objects brought back from her travels.

dividing space

Space is the essence of a loft, so do what you can to maximize it. Whether you have got a sweeping floor area of, say, 5,000 square feet (465 square metres), or somewhere much smaller, try to divide it as little as possible (see space planning, page 58) and keep the interior as uncluttered as you can.

There are clever visual tricks you can play to accentuate the size of your loft should you feel the need. Paint your walls one colour and your ceiling a shade lighter; let your flooring float rather than butt up to the walls; create a strong visual diagonal from one corner of your interior to the other to direct the eye right across the space. These may be principles that apply equally to any property but in a loft they take on an altogether larger role and the impact is far greater.

A loft is not a conventional house, so do your best not to treat it like one. You may have chosen to carve up your interior, but that doesn't mean you have to fill it with a geometry of boxy rooms and narrow corridors. Think laterally and dream up innovative and aesthetic solutions for dividing up your loft without compartmentalizing it; defining different zones for eating, bathing, working and sleeping without compromising spaciousness or limiting flexibility.

the fixed wall

If something is going to be there forever, make a feature of it. Even a prosaic partition can become a visual *tour de force* if you want it to. Once you have decided that you need some sort of fixed separating structure, don't feel you have to limit yourself to two dimensions. Think instead about creating interesting sculptural forms, which will divide up the space for you but also become a feature in themselves – particularly if you decorate them in an interesting way.

Create a snake-like plane of wall, for example, to curve sinuously between the bathroom and the living area. Do away with doors and instead erect solitary or overlapping panels of wall, which can hide a room or just a clothes rail from view but which essentially keep the space open. This can work especially well between a bedroom and an en-suite bathroom or as a means of isolating a shower without the need for a cubicle.

If you want to keep your interior as open-plan as possible and disguise the fact that you have divided up your space at all, construct a seamless wall of units all the way along one side of your loft. This will enable you to hide all your clutter from view, giving you copious amounts of space to store everything from your clothes to the kitchen sink (see Els Lybeert's loft in Ghent, page 69) and, by not intruding in any way on the rest of the interior, it will become 'invisible' when the doors are closed.

When you come to create any fixed structure in your interior, think about using unconventional and unexpected materials. Panels of sandblasted or frosted glass, for example, will look modern, blur the view of a bathroom or bedroom and let the sunlight stream in. Alternatively, for more flexibility, sandwich Priva-Lite between two panes of glass to make it clear or opaque at the flick of a switch (see page 55). For a more funky effect, use coloured laminated glass which, when the light shines through it, will give a wonderful tint to the interior (see page 16). Consider, too, constructing panels of wall in concrete, stone, wood or even metal (but first check with an expert that it is feasible to use these materials in your space).

Opposite **Think of unusual ways to divide up your space. Here, a graphic curve of sandblasted glass punched with clear glass bricks screens a shower from view but lets in light.**

Right **A half-height panel of wall can separate different parts of a loft but keep the space essentially open. Here, the shower is hidden from view without the need for a cubicle.**

Top left and right **Belgian designers Paul Ibens and Claire Bataille created a graphic, light-filled interior by using frosted glass panels and cantilevered doors to divide up the space. The kitchen, shown here, can be left open to the living area or enclosed in an opaque glass box.**

Bottom left **By placing a freestanding panel of wall at the end or the head of a bed, you can create a hidden storage area for clothes without the need for cupboards.**

sliding, folding and disappearing walls

In a loft, the best walls are those that can be there when you want them and disappear when you don't, so think about building flexible structures into your interior right at the start. A sliding panel or a cantilevered door, which can be top hung or inset into a floor track, will make a graphic partition between a bedroom and a living area, for example, and enable you to change the configuration of your space in an instant. It will also add structural and decorative interest to the interior, particularly if you experiment with a mixture of materials: perhaps metal and Perspex, or glass and wood. For an especially dramatic effect, divide private and communal space with a 'wall' of doors, which can be opened up like an Advent calendar to expose the 'rooms' behind them (see page 130) or position foldaway floor-to-ceiling doors strategically so that they enclose space to form rooms when they are open and vanish into the surrounding architecture when they are closed.

screens

Screens are a great go-anywhere solution, which can give you privacy wherever you want it. Buy ready-made screens or get them made up in a material that will suit your space: wood, fabric, frosted glass, Perspex, metal or mesh. Anything goes, but remember that the more translucent the material, the more light will shine through.

Keep the design simple, graphic and versatile. Put wheels on the bottom of a glass pane so it can easily be moved or put to one side when you don't want it; add hinges to a screen made of plywood, so it can be folded up in an instant; or use a roll-up room divider. And don't be afraid to be bold – a screen made up of panels of Perspex in different colours, for example, can provide a brilliant visual focus, and a mix of contrasting textures can work equally well. For a client's London loft, designer Ben Mathers made up mobile screens in fake suede and mirrored glass, which hid rails of clothes and created an instant dressing 'room'.

using the furniture

Another more impromptu approach to dividing up your space is simply to use the furniture. With its overblown dimensions, a loft can take overscaled furniture and any large piece, such as a bookcase, a set of freestanding shelves or even a giant sofa, can effectively separate parts of your interior. If you don't have any particularly large pieces of furniture, construct a simple room divider-cum-shelving system by stacking up simple wooden cubes to the desired height. Such a versatile solution to space separation will give you endless flexibility and – even better – additional storage. Remember, too, that the furniture itself will define the space it sits in, so you can create a sitting 'room' simply with two armchairs and a sofa without the need for walls.

Left and right **British designer Ben Mathers of CA1 created giant screens in fake suede and mirrored glass so his client could conceal his clutter and transform the layout of his space whenever he liked.**

Below **By placing two vast bookcases back to back (with a corridor between them), design consultant Naomi Cleaver effectively screened off the bedroom from the open-plan living area in her London loft.**

This New York loft has
been kept almost entirely
open-plan and the furniture
alone defines the function
of each part of the space.

blinds, curtains and drapes

Conventional window treatments can work just as well within the interior of a loft as around its glassy perimeter. Blinds, for example, provide simple, streamlined screening for an internal window or a glass wall between 'rooms'. Venetian blinds make a particularly graphic partition, bringing strong geometric pattern to a minimal space when they are open and giving total privacy when they are closed.

Curtains, too, can work well inside your space. Not only can they provide a bit of extra insulation (as long as they are reasonably thick), they will also give a touch of softness to the most rectilinear interior. Use them to screen off a mezzanine, a bedroom area or even just a bed. For maximum versatility, make sure they are easy to open and close in an instant (a hidden track works well). If your loft is fairly dark and you are anxious to maximize natural light, choose a diaphanous fabric for your curtains, such as muslin, calico or a synthetic sheer. These may not give you complete privacy but they will let in the sunlight. If, on the other hand, you are after a funky, modern look, choose interesting and unexpected materials, such as coloured plastic ribbon, woven metal, fluffy fleece or glossy PVC.

If you have finished decorating your loft and suddenly realize you need to separate your working area, say, from your living area, don't despair. By pinning up casual, impromptu drapes you can create a fluid and flexible partition that can easily be taken down when you want the open space back again (see designer Peter Wylly's loft, pages 80–1). You can create instant drapes very cheaply by hanging simple panels of material from hooks attached to the ceiling. Stagger the position of them and use different lengths, textures and colours of fabric for alternative effects. A series of brightly coloured sheers, for example, will make a hanging work of art and also give an appealingly diffused quality to the light in the interior. Keep up to date, if you like, by changing the fabric from season to season.

Curtains can work brilliantly inside a loft space. Here, a length of light, diaphanous fabric gives a soft edge to the bedroom and provides privacy without closing the space in.

A bedroom that **moves**, an office that **swivels**, a **room** with a view that can **change** in an instant ... freewheeling **capsule living** is the shape of things to come.

living pods

For the most dynamic space-divider of all, create a room within a room by tucking a bedroom or an office area into a self-contained capsule or pod. This will allow you to keep your interior open plan while at the same time giving you the freedom to devise individual, room-based decorating schemes. It will also enable you to create the ultimate designated area, keeping your work, for example, entirely separate from the rest of the living space.

Art teacher Els Lybeert came up with a brilliant version of the pod in her loft in the Belgian port of Ghent. Wanting to give her children a bit of private space but at the same time maintain a free-flowing open-plan interior, she created very basic, giant wooden boxes and put them on castors. Like mini mobile homes

with their own window and two sliding doors, these boxes can be wheeled anywhere in the loft. They give the children the flexibility of having separate rooms or – by putting them alongside each other with the doors open – creating one larger, shared space. An ingenious combination of the functional and the fun, this solution also allowed Lybeert's children to express themselves however they liked inside their 'rooms' without disrupting the subtlety of the overall decorative scheme.

This kind of freewheeling pod would work best in a large loft where its potential could be maximized and where it would not look out of place or awkward. In a smaller loft, built-in pods are better and can make a great self-contained space for an office or simply a bed.

Opposite **With their bedrooms contained in giant mobile boxes, Els Lybeert's children can decorate them as they like without disrupting the overall scheme.**

Next page **The living pods can be wheeled around at whim whenever the children want a change of scene. They can even be put together to create one larger shared space.**

choosing your palette

Colour is the most versatile, visual and expressive of decorating tools with the power to transform everything about a space from the sense of proportion to the chill factor. According to colour therapists, it can even influence our mood. Blue is calming; yellow, energizing; red, great for stirring up passion. To make it work well, colour needs to be used wisely and imaginatively, particularly in a loft where overscaled dimensions and lack of conventional barriers mean any colour scheme will have a massive impact.

In the past, many have chosen to avoid the issue altogether by keeping that ex-industrial all-white look. It is dramatic, of course; it will maximize light and provide a good clean backdrop to any interior; but it is not – dare I say it – very adventurous and will do nothing to warm, soften or animate your space (all major considerations in a loft). By using colour cleverly you can do all these things and more. You can highlight the good points of your space and camouflage the bad. You can, in the absence of rooms, define different zones of your interior and colour-connect one with another. Best of all, colour allows you to bring personality and individuality to your loft cheaply, easily and relatively quickly.

what colours to use

Before you pick a colour scheme, consider the bare bones of your loft. Is it flooded with natural light or in need of brightening up? Is it comfortable and personable or somewhere that is crying out for warmth? Choose colours that will give you whatever feel you are after and, before you commit yourself, buy sample pots of paint and swatches of fabric and flooring to see which work best where. Remember, too, that natural light will transform colour, so whatever shades you pick for the brightest part of your loft will change throughout the day. Most important of all, select shades you can live with. Aubergine may be all the rage in the latest magazines but it might not be right for you.

If you are in two minds, feel free to mix colours – two-tone interiors can work well (think camel and sky blue; chocolate and gourd green; black and white) – but be careful, particularly in a completely open-plan space, not to choose tones that jar with each other. That doesn't mean you have to be subtle, however. Big spaces can take big colour, so don't be afraid to be bold. Just remember that dark colours will make your interior seem smaller.

Left **The owner of this apartment used a Swedish-inspired palette of blues, greys and greens across everything from walls to floors to doors.**

Opposite **Each different part of the interior is defined with a slightly different tone of colour, but the overall effect is one of striking unity.**

where to use colour

Although there are endless principles dictating which colours to use where (particularly if you are decorating your interior to Feng Shui guidelines, see page 80), the best advice is to do whatever feels and looks right to you. Colour is an emotive thing and, while you should be aware of the effects certain shades will create in certain places, you should not feel bound by convention.

You might choose to wash your entire interior with raw and vivid pigments or opt for a more subtle colour overall and use one or two vivid tones as a highlight, in the furnishings or accessories, for example. You might decide to use panels of different colours on the walls or the floors, or resolve to keep the surface of your loft sophisticatedly neutral (white, even) and only use bolder colours in secret spaces, such as the inside of a cupboard door or on the walls of a shower (see page 173). This technique allows you to use as brilliant shades as you like without worrying about them clashing with the furniture and – once discovered – their impact will be all the greater.

creating 'rooms' with colour

An open-plan interior can lack definition and seem bland if the walls, floor and ceiling are all the same colour. One way to avoid this is to create 'rooms' with the use of colour, defining separate zones or areas of your loft with different shades so the eye can easily differentiate between them. Paint your living space yellow, for example, and your sleeping area green or use two tones of flooring to divide the private parts of your loft from the communal. Colour-coding your space in this way will make it visually interesting and give

Katleen Van Zandtweghe turned a giant juice and lemonade factory in Belgium into a temple of colour, using a different slice of the spectrum for each area. The winter room (opposite) is like an abstract painting with its geometric blocks of fuchsia, peach and crimson; an effect exaggerated by the giant doorways which punctuate the interior, framing colourful vistas of every room (right).

Next page **A moodier colour scheme can have as much impact but works best in a bright, sun-filled loft.**

it a cohesion that it might otherwise lack (particularly if you use a unifying highlight colour across the whole of the interior). It will also allow you to identify the function of a particular part of the loft without building physical barriers and disrupting the free-flowing space.

the one-colour look

If you do decide to create 'rooms' of colour, why not take the idea as far as it will go by taking different tones of the same colour across everything from walls to floors to tableware? In a kitchen, for example, use the same shade of green in the Formica of the tabletop and the rubber of the floor, the same colour paint in matt finish on the walls and gloss finish on the units, and choose accessories that are just a

degree or two lighter or darker than your chosen key shade. This kind of wraparound tonal effect is visually very striking and brings a strong sense of unity to the disparate elements of any space – especially one that is as open and unconstrained as a loft.

For inspiration, take a look at Katleen Van Zandtweghe's loft in an old juice factory in Belgium (opposite and above). She created a brilliant, graphic and logical decorative scheme by using different slices of the colour spectrum in each part of her loft: pink, fuchsia, crimson and scarlet for the winter living room and varying tones of green for the sitting area, for example. While Katleen chose to use vivid colours, the same idea would work just as effectively with more subtle, muted tones.

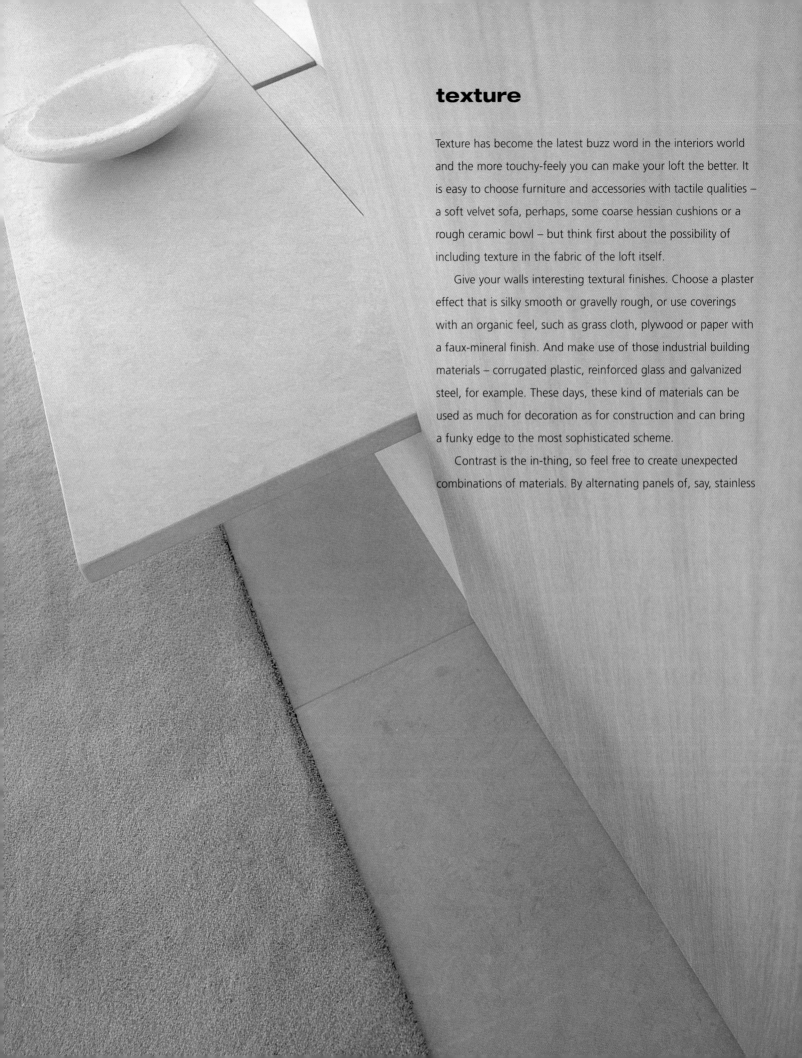

texture

Texture has become the latest buzz word in the interiors world and the more touchy-feely you can make your loft the better. It is easy to choose furniture and accessories with tactile qualities – a soft velvet sofa, perhaps, some coarse hessian cushions or a rough ceramic bowl – but think first about the possibility of including texture in the fabric of the loft itself.

Give your walls interesting textural finishes. Choose a plaster effect that is silky smooth or gravelly rough, or use coverings with an organic feel, such as grass cloth, plywood or paper with a faux-mineral finish. And make use of those industrial building materials – corrugated plastic, reinforced glass and galvanized steel, for example. These days, these kind of materials can be used as much for decoration as for construction and can bring a funky edge to the most sophisticated scheme.

Contrast is the in-thing, so feel free to create unexpected combinations of materials. By alternating panels of, say, stainless steel and fake suede or glass and wood you will draw attention to their very different textures and, at the same time, achieve a cutting-edge look. Contrasts of texture can work at a more subtle level, too. Even by combining the gloss and matt finishes of the same paint colour on a wall (in horizontal or vertical stripes, for example), you will get a striking and tactile effect.

For floors, particularly, texture is vital, so choose your materials carefully and be aware of the vastly different looks you can create depending on what you select (see page 132). Mix the rough with the smooth; the hard with the soft and be as experimental as you dare. Lay sleek limestone slabs alongside the deepest, softest carpet; use grainy slate against pearly marble; rubber against steel. Make sure, above all, that your flooring feels as good as it looks.

These days, homes are more about soul than style; comfort than designer cachet. By maximizing texture throughout the interior of your loft, you can transform any sterile ex-industrial space into a sensual sanctuary from the urban world outside.

multipurpose areas

Areas that can double up – a kitchen that you can entertain in, for example, or a guest bedroom that can turn into an office – seem the ideal solution for modern living. As our lifestyles become increasingly informal and unpredictable, we no longer want to split our homes into a series of one-function rooms that may never get used. Instead, we want to create fewer, combination or transformable spaces that can play more than one role and adapt to suit our changing needs. By reducing our requirement for rooms in this way, we also, of course, maximize the potential for acres of unsullied space.

Nowhere is it easier to try out this new integrated way of living than a loft where, more often than not, you are building an interior from scratch. Freed from the constraints of an existing layout of rooms, you can do just what you like with your space and create as many multipurpose areas as you need.

Consider, first, just how integrated you would like your interior to be. If you simply want one enormous space where you can do everything, keep the layout as open-plan as you can and come up with a cohesive decorative scheme that will bring all the disparate elements together. Treat the space like one room not a series of separate ones and use generic furniture that is not room specific. What you should look for are pieces that can adapt to a number of functions (the dining table at which you can work or entertain, for example) and won't look out of place wherever you choose to put them.

Creating this kind of flexibility is just as important if you are only going multipurpose on a smaller scale – creating a guest-bedroom-cum-home-office, for example, as below. The key is to keep the decorative scheme simple and understated so that the room can seamlessly swap its functions when you want it to transfer from one role to another. To make things even easier for yourself, incorporate foldaway fixtures and fittings into the structure of the room itself – a bed that folds down from the wall, for example, or a flap-down desk – and buy furniture on castors so that you can wheel it in or out as you please. Most important of all, make sure you have enough storage space to allow you to hide the computer, the printer and the fax machine from view when your friends come to stay.

In this small London loft, an ingenious folding wall, which can be opened up as much or as little as required, divides the private space from the communal.

A fold-down bed, built into the structure of the interior right at the start, gives the owner the flexibility to change the function of the room in an instant.

flooring

Getting the flooring right is fundamental to the success of any interior but is particularly key in a loft where the largely undivided expanse of floor is likely to be bigger and more exposed than in a conventional house. Without rooms, there is no formula to fall back on – linoleum for kitchens, carpet for sitting rooms, quarry tiles for halls – and while this can seem daunting, it is also liberating to realize that anything goes. Alongside all the traditional favourites – stone, wood, carpet, tiles – is a host of new possibilities, such as metal, concrete, plastic and rubber. The loft has brought these staples of the industrial world into the domestic interior and nowhere do they seem more at home.

First, consider the practicalities. Will bamboo matting cope with your underfloor heating? Will peach rubber tiles withstand kitchen stains? Can you afford to lay limestone over 5,000 square feet (465 square metres)? Think about the requirements of your space and the limitations of your budget and then consider ways of achieving the look you want within those constraints.

hard flooring

stone

It is hard to beat the smoothness of stone underfoot (especially when it is warmed by underfloor heating) and this most ancient of flooring materials will bring a feeling of permanence and integrity to the most ephemeral interior. Because it works well, practically and aesthetically, anywhere from the bathroom to the bedroom, it is perfect for a loft. Using giant slabs of one kind of stone

A stripped wooden floor brings softness and warmth to an ex-industrial space, whether you choose a pale, natural look (above) or a glowing honey tone (right). It will also work well with any furniture - traditional, ethnic or modern.

throughout your space will unify any decorative scheme (although, as with any natural material, you will get variations in colour and texture); using a mixture of stones – pearly travertine for the bedroom, for example, and flat matt slate for the bathroom – allows you to create interesting textural contrasts.

Bought new, high-quality stone doesn't come cheap, but it should last a lifetime. Alternatively, scour salvage yards for less expensive old stone slabs, which will give your interior instant patina, or think of ways of creating the same sleek effect using different, less costly materials. Concrete, for example, makes a good alternative to stone and will give a modern, funky edge to your space. Remember, though, that as it is porous, it will need to be sealed before use and also may have to be cast on site.

wood

A sweep of grainy wood will bring instant warmth to the most sterile ex-industrial interior and make a perfect foil to any shade of walls. Choose wood with a tone that suits your space – honey-coloured beech or birch for a light contemporary look or a richer-coloured hardwood, such as cherry or walnut, for a moodier modern feel. Don't worry about selecting planks that all look the same – any knots and grain will add texture and character to your floor. Keep your laying schemes simple; fancy parquet patterns can look fussy used over a large area and the wood itself should provide all the decoration you need.

High-quality wooden flooring is expensive, so look out for old boards – such as reclaimed oak or old teak – which should be cheaper (but don't expect rock-bottom prices) and also look nicely timeworn. Or, consider ways of achieving a similar effect on a smaller budget. Although their life span will be shorter, plywood, wood laminates and even varnished hardboard are fair substitutes if they are finished well and laid interestingly (in big square slabs with bevelled edges, for example).

metal & glass

Perfect for an industrial look, metal flooring is durable, practical and need not cost you a fortune. Use aluminium tread on the stairs (if you have any) or stainless steel floor tiles in the kitchen. It will look modern, reflect the light and, if you have underfloor heating, act like a giant radiator. Glass will give you a brilliantly

see-through floor and instant drama, but it is pricey and needs to be individually specified to make sure it will meet loading requirements. Get expert advice on what glass to use and how to fit it.

medium-weight flooring
linoleum, rubber & vinyl

The most flexible of all the flooring fabrics, linoleum, rubber and vinyl are brilliant for loft spaces and provide an instant cover-up for floors that are less than perfect. They are soft, uniform and comfortable underfoot and also come in countless colours and designs. Use vinyls that emulate wood or stone, metal or glass, or create your own patterns (although custom-made flooring will cost you). Mix and match rubber tiles in different colours or contrasting textures. This kind of flooring doesn't come cheap, but it is practical, hard-wearing (remember: the thicker it is, the longer it will last) and supremely versatile.

natural fibres & leather

Great for adding instant texture to any space, 'natural flooring' has been the hit of the 1990s and can work well in a loft space. It is not, however, suitable for hard-working or humid areas, such as the kitchen or the bathroom, so if you want uniform flooring throughout your loft, it is not for you. Leather, too, is unsuitable for utility areas, but makes for a very luxurious, tactile bedroom floor and should improve with age.

soft flooring
carpet

Carpet may not have had a good press in recent years, but the best beats other flooring hands down for softness, warmth and comfort. Like natural flooring, carpet is unsuitable for kitchens and bathrooms but can transform a living area or a bedroom into the ultimate comfort zone. These days, carpet comes in virtually any shade from subtle neutrals to brilliant primaries. Choose colours that complement your interior, but be as bold and inventive as you dare and feel free to mix colours and create graphic and fluid patterns with two or more shades. Quality will out, so buy the best carpet you can afford and, most importantly, feel it underfoot before you take it home and choose textures that will make you want to throw off your shoes.

rugs

A cheaper and more versatile alternative to wall-to-wall carpeting, the rug has been around for centuries and never lost its appeal. Bringing instant colour and texture to any interior, a rug works particularly well in a loft space, where it breaks up what can be a relentless sweep of the same flooring, and can be moved to wherever you need it. Choose a design that will suit your space and a texture that is softer than soft.

creating rooms with flooring

As with your use of colour (see page 122), by using different materials for your flooring or laying patterns, you can visually separate the different areas of your loft without the need for dividing walls or screens. The living area could be stone, for example, but the dining space within that could be carpeted; the general floor could be wooden but the kitchen area could be laid in a horizontal or diagonal grain to the rest to make it stand out.

To maximize this effect, you can also raise the level of the floor for such 'internal' areas, thereby creating platforms that define the different zones of your loft. These can be any shape you choose; for something dramatic, lay stainless steel floor tiles, cut into curvy, organic shapes, on top of your general flooring (whether it is wood, concrete, linoleum or carpet) to define the kitchen. For something more subtle, use the gloss and matt finishes of the same colour paint on a floor.

Opposite **Made of poured cement, finished with many coats of grey paint, this floor is practical, durable and would give a sleek, modern look to any interior.**

Below **Mosaic is great for adding colour and patina to an interior but, as it is pricey and time-consuming to lay, it is best used for small areas, such as a bathroom.**

windows

Windows are what lofts are all about: giant sweeps of glass that stretch all the way from floor to ceiling; enormous openings that summon in the sunlight and give wide-angle views over the city. They are the eyes and soul of the place and, for some, the most appealing feature, so when you are laying out your interior do your best to maximize their impact (see space planning, page 58).

It is one thing to show off your industrial-scale assets, however, and quite another to leave them entirely bare. While loft-living purists may blanch at the very thought of window treatments, you may find that creating some sort of screen is essential. Lofts, as a rule, have a vast expanse of window – sometimes even more than wall – so unless your building is the tallest on the block and is not overlooked by others, you and your interior will be very much exposed to public view. And this is a problem that works both ways. As lofts are often located in developing areas of cities, you might find that you want to be able to draw the blinds and screen your view of the surrounding piles of rubble, bricks and builders. Then, of course, there is the weather to think about. Giant

Opposite left **The owner of this New York loft has left the giant windows completely bare, allowing sunlight to pour into the interior and giving her framed views of the surrounding cityscape.**

Opposite top right **Windows with an unusual shape should be made a feature of, and here, a New York loft dweller has maximized the impact of hers by using furniture that echoes their form.**

Opposite bottom right **Ornamental windows give you a decorative feature on a plate, so relish them.**

Left **Internal windows can bring light to the darkest parts of an interior. In this London loft, medieval-style slits cast shards of sunlight across the back bedroom.**

windows can make for chilly interiors in the winter, so you will need to think about insulation. Conversely, in the summer, you may find the quantity of unremitting heat and light which stream through the windows simply too much for you (particularly if your loft faces south). Some sort of cover-up is the answer but it can be difficult to know quite where to begin. The industrial-scale dimensions of the windows make conventional curtaining solutions impractical and they would simply look wrong (nothing, it seems, would be more out of a place in a loft than a pelmet). Scour magazines for ideas and think about the kind of look you are after. And remember, whatever you choose, keep it simple and flexible, and don't shut out the light.

the soft stuff

Lofts are not the place for swags and frills, but curtains can work (and provide a bit of insulation) if you keep them understated and graphic. Don't feel you have to make them full-length (if your windows are particularly large, it would cost you a fortune). Belgian architect Vincent Van Duysen, for example, hung simple cream cotton drapes from rods placed halfway up his windows, giving him privacy but not obscuring his views of the sky (see page 43). For a more modern look, use Perspex rods or thick wire instead of metal or wood; or attach the fabric in a novel way, with plastic or aluminium pegs, perhaps, or with fishing line threaded through eyelets.

Think up unconventional ways to screen your windows – if you need to – without blocking out the light. Pieces of coloured vinyl film can create a graphic chequerboard effect (left) and be changed when you get bored with them. Similarly, opaque paper or plastic, simply stuck to the window will make an effective and flexible screen (opposite).

Below **New Yorker Neil Zukerman made the most of the light in his SoHo loft by using the window ledge to display his collection of oversized scent bottles.**

When it comes to choosing the fabric, consider the sunlight. Diaphanous materials are best as they will filter the light, giving it a soft, diffused quality that is lovely to live with. And think about the colour. Brilliant sheers work well and look good layered one on top of the other; plain and simple calicos and cottons are hard to beat for a natural look. Choose something you like and that works well with the general colour scheme.

the hard stuff

If the very thought of furnishings makes you go cold, consider creating more structural screening solutions. If your loft is at street level, you can replace the lower panes with frosted glass or use some sort of spray-on screening device. While these techniques will give you privacy, however, they will also permanently obscure your view. For more flexibility, fix panels of sandblasted glass or coloured Perspex on tracks in front of your windows (just to head height is fine). These will screen you from view and soften the light but can be opened and closed as you please.

blinds

Unfussy and graphic, blinds work well in a loft. If you want to maximize light, remember to choose a pale colour or a diaphanous material, or buy a pierced blind that will let shards of sunlight through the holes. Consider, too, covering the bottom half of the window so you can have privacy without entirely shutting out the sky. If, on the other hand, you are worried about too much light, layer one or more simple blinds on top of each other to give you varying degrees of screening and the flexibility to change the mood of your interior instantaneously (if you want total darkness, make one layer a black-out blind). Venetian blinds also work well in a loft space and have the benefit, when open, of casting wonderfully geometric shadows on the floor.

the inventive

Unconventional windows can take unconventional treatment. Cover up your panes with transparent vinyl film or tissue paper for a colourful effect that is easy to change when you tire of it. And for curtains, think about using unexpected materials, such as woven aluminium for the ultimate industrial look, utilitarian sail fabric or cosy fleece for instant warmth.

windows are the eyes

Opposite **Following the linear look of this Eastern-style dining area, a Venetian blind has been used to screen the window and bring geometric pattern to a minimal space.**

Right **By using lengths of graphic Vivienne Westwood fabric, the owners of this East London loft have made a funky decorative feature out of their curtains.**

Below **In this sleek and minimal modern interior, natural light has been maximized by a white colour scheme and an emphasis on shiny, reflective surfaces.**

Opposite **Two graphic Jack Lights by designer Tom Dixon make an alternative support for a glass tabletop and create a brilliant visual focus.**

lighting

The quality and quantity of natural light that you get in ex-industrial spaces is what drew New York's artists to them in the first place, but it is a mistake to think that every corner of a loft will automatically be flooded with sunlight. The biggest lofts – those that take up an entire floor of an old warehouse or factory – will have a very deep floor area and, even if the windows are huge, natural light will not be able to penetrate across the entire space. A smaller loft may only have windows on one side and while it may be bright at the front, the internal spaces at the back may be dark throughout the day. No interior will look good without suitable lighting and what you need is a scheme that

does everything it can to maximize natural light but which also supplements it with a system of artificial lights that can come into play as and when you need it.

maximizing natural light

Make the most of the sunlight that pours in through the windows. Use screening devices that don't block out the light (see windows, page 136); make any internal walls or barriers out of transparent materials; and use see-through furniture and accessories wherever you can. If you are on the top of the building, put in skylights. If not, think about creating internal windows that will let shards of

sunlight through. Your choice of materials can make a difference, too: stainless steel and mirrored glass reflect the light, and any light varnished surface will work better than a dark matt one.

using artificial light

It is worth spending time and a little money getting your lighting right. What you are after is the flexibility to change the mood of your interior whenever you want to, so consider how this can best be achieved in your particular space and create a system that works for you. If your loft is naturally bright, consider that daylight is very blue and may need to be balanced with warm tungsten light. If, by contrast, you want to cool your space down, introduce daylight simulators.

Changes in the time of day or the season will be much more noticeable in a loft than in a conventional house, and an adaptable lighting system can make allowances for this. One idea is to have a double layer of lighting: one to act as a lighting canvas (a series of mood lighting on dimmers) and the other to highlight particular areas (task lighting), giving you endless permutations to play with.

Different parts of your loft will, of course, have different lighting requirements. In the kitchen, you will need strong and effective task lighting – spots or strips – over the worktop, cooker and sink; in the dining area and bedroom, ambient lighting (achieved with dimmers, drop or wall lights) is more suitable. To cope with the variety of your lighting needs, it makes sense to create some sort of integrated system, but whatever you choose, make sure it is easy to control and not overcomplicated and, keep your switches to a minimum so that you don't forget which is for what.

Top left **Don't simply view lighting in functional terms; make a feature of it by using unexpected fixtures and fittings. In his New York loft, Neil Zukerman created an installation of neon strips as an ironic reference to the urban streets outside.**

Left and opposite **Above all, fill your interior with lights that you like, regardless of their period. Ethnic lanterns brought back from abroad or a quirky collection of old-fashioned lamps will give an individual stamp to the most modern loft space.**

creating rooms with light

Like flooring and colour, light is a useful tool for defining the different zones within a loft space, particularly if it is largely open-plan. You can highlight some areas with bright lights and isolate others with more subtle low lighting. To vary the atmosphere you can also create intimate 'pools' of light, which will draw the eye to a particular part of your loft or even just a piece of furniture or art. Most of all, be creative with your lighting – just because you are dealing with something functional, doesn't mean you can't be imaginative, too.

making a feature of light

Employed ingeniously, lighting can become very much part of a decorative scheme. If you have freestanding lamps, make them sculptural or quirky and interesting so they become a feature, and use standard fittings in unexpected ways. A bunch of bare bulbs or a graphic row of neon strips, for example, will take on a presence that the single versions never could. Treat light as you would any other material and manipulate it creatively. Install downlighters to cast overlapping arches of light on a wall, perhaps, or use coloured light to highlight elements of the interior.

How to be **clutter-free** is the preoccupation of the age
and **storage** is the solution, enabling you to **create** the
perfect modern, **minimalist** interior, with all your
belongings concealed behind **sleek** cupboard doors.

storage

In any modern interior, storage is key. It alone allows us to create
the streamlined, clutter-free, minimalist spaces we crave by providing
somewhere to stow away the mountains of stuff we accumulate
in our daily lives. You simply can't have too much of it.

If you are building your loft from scratch, incorporate as
much storage as you can into the architecture of the space itself.
Construct a streamlined wall of cupboards along one side of your
loft, put part of your interior on a platform to give you storage
space underneath and make good use of any dead space (old
lift shafts, understairs areas, etc.) for cupboards or shelves.
Think, too, about exploiting those high ceilings. Two ingenious
architecture students in London put their dining table on a pulley
system so that it could be lowered when they were entertaining
or whisked up to the ceiling when it was not in use.* If you create
comprehensive storage from the word go, you will save yourself
money: not only are built-in fittings tax-free, they will also reduce
your requirement for freestanding furniture.

If you have bought a loft that has already been designed by
a developer, storage should come with it. If there is not enough
for your needs choose furniture that doubles up (see page 150),
make use of any available unseen space (under the bed, for
example), and be inventive. Storage doesn't need to be
sophisticated. Create your own impromptu system with anything
that comes to hand – vegetable crates and shoe boxes, etc. – or
cover a wall with hooks so you can hang up storage bags.
Choose furnishings, too, that do two things at once. Use vinyl
CD holders as screens, for example, or put up a pocket-covered
shower curtain to store all those bathroom bottles.

However good your system is, of course, it will only work if
you want it to. If all else fails, put all your stuff in storage and
play at being a true minimalist. You might find you like it.

Opposite **This New York loft
was constructed with a
vast walk-in wardrobe so
that the adjacent rooms
could be kept free of
clothes and clutter.**

Below **In this Zukerman
loft the overflow from the
giant built-in bookcases is
simply piled up on a stool.**

...bedroom toy chest the
ultimate fashion item
design comes in countless
colours, sizes and shapes.

Far right A simple built-in
storage system such as
this makes it easy to keep
clutter at a minimum and
shoes under control.

furniture

Moving into a loft for the first time can mean radically rethinking your furniture. Pieces that might have fit perfectly in an ordinary house will not necessarily work in a space carved out of an old industrial or commercial building. Altogether looser, more informal and more open than a conventional home, a loft cries out for flexible furniture that is not room-dependent; go-anywhere pieces that will look good wherever you choose to put them. Before you buy, consider what you need in terms of colour, size and shape, and don't be tempted to overfill your space – a few functional pieces should be all you need.

built-in furniture

Get as much furniture built into your loft as you can. Pull-down desks, storage drawers and foldaway beds can take the place of freestanding pieces and will enable you to keep your living space clear and clean. They will also give you the flexibility to change the function of a room in an instant.

go-anywhere furniture

Choose furniture that looks good anywhere so you can change the look of the place as often as you like. A suede cube seat will work just as well in the living area as the bedroom (and will make a great coffee table, too). Narrow wooden consoles can be pushed together for an impromptu dining table, but would not look out of place in an office space or a dressing room. A beanbag will be at home everywhere. Put simple furniture on castors (or buy ready-made mobile pieces) so you can wheel them around your loft and reconfigure the place at whim.

furniture that doubles up

In a loft, less is very definitely more, so in order not to fill up your space with furniture, try to choose pieces that perform two functions at once. Make your dining table large enough to work at, buy a box-bench that has a hollow interior for storing clutter or construct a low shelf that can be used as a seat or a stacking space along one wall of your loft. Think laterally; even the most mundane household items – packing crates or vegetable pallets, for example – can be dual-purpose and put to good use.

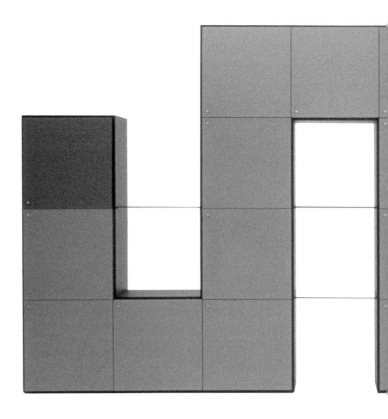

modular furniture

Responding to the loft dwellers' need for flexibility, designers are increasingly coming up with ideas for adaptable furniture that can be configured in a number of different ways – the expanding book shelf, which pivots into a screen-cum-room divider; the table made up of blocks, which slot together to give five or six different results. Brilliantly versatile, this kind of modular furniture is hard to beat for a loft space because it can be adapted to suit any location or situation.

industrial furniture

An ex-industrial space cries out for things that hint at the history of the building and, thanks to lofts, old factory fittings have become the new domestic must-haves, bringing cool industrial highlights to the most refined interiors with anything from salvaged iron radiators to steel storage racks on wheels. You don't have to limit yourself to the purely industrial; any utilitarian object will lend your living space instant street cred. Try

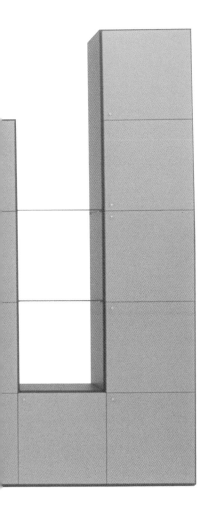

hospital trolleys (great for the base of a dining table); old shop showcases (good for storage), photographers' sinks; or simply a row of white plastic buckets. Old office fittings, too, will fit the aesthetic: metal filing cabinets (resprayed in colours that suit your space) or 1950s and 1960s swivel chairs. If you can't find original pieces, buy new stuff made with industrial materials – concrete or scaffolding poles.

overscaled furniture

Furniture that looks huge in a conventional house will be dwarfed by the vast dimensions of most loft spaces, so you may need to buy some industrial-scale items to furnish your new interior. While giant pieces can lend instant drama to your space, don't forget that you may well have to get them custom-made and big things invariably cost big money. Consider, too,

Above **Masters of the modular, Edra have devised this new Paesaggi Italiani furnishing system whose basic components can be arranged in a multitude of ways.**

Above **Called l'Homme et la Femme, this white modular sofa, also by Edra, can be manipulated into a variety of different shapes to suit every occasion.**

Left **Expandable furniture works well in any loft. This pivoting book shelf opens up to make a screen-cum-room divider with twice the storage space.**

that if you move back to a conventional house in the future, it is unlikely you will be able to take these large pieces with you.

incidental furniture

One way to keep your home as clear and clutter-free as possible is to have a selection of simple, impromptu furniture that can be brought out as and when you need it – like the 'occasional' table in times gone by. Instead of extra armchairs and sofas, choose unstructured pieces, such as beanbags and large squashy floor cushions, which can be bundled out of sight into a cupboard when they are not needed, or simple mattresses covered in tactile fabrics like fake suede, fur, raw silk or velvet, which can easily be stowed under a bed when not in use. Not only will these give you extra seating anywhere you want it, they will also give your interior a funky, informal feel. They can also be re-covered easily and inexpensively when you feel like a change of fabric.

a little of what you like

Do not fall into the trap of furnishing your loft in a formulaic way; fill it, above all, with things you like and feel comfortable with. If you are a fan of Louis XV gilded chairs or ornate antique headboards, indulge your passion. An unexpected touch of grandeur can look brilliant in the rawest space. Decorating a loft should be the ultimate vehicle for self-expression, so don't let your creativity be stifled by convention.

architectonic furniture

This is furniture as sculpture; the single piece that makes a big statement and helps to define all that empty space. It could be a curvy, colourful sofa in a giant white loft or a gilded spiral light in a minimal, monochrome apartment; it could be a 20-foot (6-metre) high carved Balinese door. Choose something, at any rate, with a big wow factor.

Opposite **New Yorker Cheryl Henson has brought an organic, natural touch to her urban loft space by filling it with furniture made from twisting, pale wood branches.**

Top right **A grand wooden day bed contrasts with New York's urban landscape.**

Bottom right **Old cinema seats make original and alternative armchairs.**

the industrial look

Whether you have bought a loft in an old flour warehouse, a nineteenth-century school or a 1970s office block, the bare bones of the space should have something of the industrial about them. There should be giant windows, high ceilings and a vast sweep of floor. There may also be more specific industrial features, such as a freight lift or an overscaled door with heavy iron hinges. These are the elements that define a loft, and while you naturally will want to make your interior comfortable and domestic, that doesn't mean you can't also celebrate its industrial past by showing off these features as much as you can.

The best way to keep a sense of the history of your space is to change as little of the existing structure as possible. Leave as much of the original shell exposed as you can, whether it is bare brick, iron pipes or peeling wallpaper. Of course you can clean this framework up before you create your interior (by sandblasting your bricks, for example) or even cover it up with some sort of floating wall or see-through facade, but don't be tempted to make the raw space too refined. For an industrial look, rough and ready is what you are after and a certain time-worn appearance is something to be relished. So, too, are quirky industrial features and if you have any old steel ladders or pulleys, for example, take them to the max.

If your loft space has few industrial features, get the look by incorporating industrial materials into the interior yourself. These days, factory basics such as steel, glass, rubber and aluminium are de rigueur in the home and builders' materials, such as concrete and even scaffolding poles, are gaining popularity by the day. Scour the catalogues of builders' suppliers to find unusual utilitarian elements which you can use in the construction or just the decoration of your space (and see industrial furniture, page 150).

Make the most of any industrial feature in your loft, whether it is the steel support of an old school gym (right) or simply an old cast-iron radiator (left).

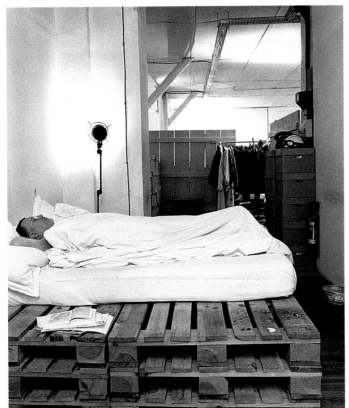

Also, search in salvage yards for interesting industrial pieces and don't worry too much about their pedigree. You may not be living in the premises of an old architecture firm in SoHo, but a salvaged architect's desk or chair, for example, will give your loft space a quirky utilitarian edge.

With this look, you can do as little or as much as you like. You could incorporate just a few factory fittings to bring an unexpectedly raw edge to a sophisticated scheme or go all out for a more extreme effect, like cutting-edge fashion designer Jean Colonna whose Parisian loft is made up entirely of industrial and utilitarian materials. Leaving the bare bones of the interior more or less as they were, he then added the occasional untreated concrete partition and furnished the space with a random collection of industrial and found objects, from metal shelving to cardboard boxes and shopping carts.

Rather than buying in the latest must-have furniture, fashion designer Jean Colonna furnished his loft with industrial shelving units and simple wooden pallets to keep the place as unrefined as possible.

Treat your **terrace** like an outdoor **room** and plan it as carefully as you do your interior to create a secret **oasis of calm**, where you can **revive** your **spirits** and enjoy the panoramic **view**.

the great outdoors

What a house in the suburbs can offer you that a loft never can is, of course, a garden. While detractors single this out as a major stumbling block to inner-city living, they fail to highlight the advantages. There is no mowing to be done; no slugs to exterminate; no wildlife to keep you awake at night. And while your rural compatriots have acres of outdoor space to roam around you have acres of space indoors. 'We have room to run and jump and ride a bike whatever the weather,' say London-based designers Steve Bowkett and Jane Tankard. 'Our total space is 2,313 square feet (215 square metres), about the plot of a typical terraced house and garden. We will simply bring the garden into the room itself.'

If you are someone who has opted to live in a loft, the chances are that you are more of an urban soul than a rural one, but if you do find yourself hankering after a bit of nature, don't despair. There are countless ways to bring a bit of the great outdoors to the most metropolitan locations.

If you are lucky and have bought a loft on the top floor of a building, you may have a roof terrace – those secret oases of calm that give panoramic views over the city and, best of all, are generally not overlooked. Treat your terrace

Left **Contrasting textures and sculptural shapes look just as good outdoors as in. A simple pile of pebbles, for example, will add an instant decorative touch.**

Right **With the same flooring and only a giant glass facade to separate them, indoor and outdoor space merge on this sun-struck Belgian rooftop.**

like an outdoor 'room' and plan it as carefully as you do your interior. This doesn't mean you have to be good at gardening. If you have little time or inclination to spend on watering and pruning, think up a scheme that is simple and low-maintenance but looks good, too. Mix pots of hardy, sculptural plants with graphic piles of pebbles; lay an area of decking for outdoor lounging or even sow your terrace with grass seed for a high-rise meadow. However, if you are planning to plant anything heavy on the terrace, get advice first so you don't end up with a hole in the ceiling.

If you do not have a roof terrace, there are many inventive ways to bring the outdoors inside. Plant window boxes with flowers, grasses (wheat is all the rage), vegetables or herbs, and if your windows don't have sills, display the boxes on the floor (if the plants are tall enough, they can even be used to divide up space). Make full use of the sunlight that streams in by turning one area of your loft into an internal greenhouse and introduce a

water feature, which will not only give you the look but the sound of nature, too.

If, however, you are in no way green-fingered, forget the planting scheme and simply use natural objects in the decoration of your loft. Don't try to be too sophisticated; the simpler and more impromptu it looks, the better. Create a display of pebbles, perhaps, or prop a graphic length of mossy bark or grainy driftwood against a wall. These rough, natural elements – used effectively – will instantly give your loft the 'soul' element that the style-conscious are striving for, and also make a rustic counterbalance to the urban, utilitarian feel of the place. One leading London advertising director, took this idea to extremes by installing an entire tree in his perpendicular loft. The tree 'grew' from the office on the bottom floor, through the bedroom (the branches became the posts of a four-poster bed) and up to the sitting room on the second floor where smaller branches were hung with a canopy of carved metal leaves.

Left **By making one of his walls a vast window, Jan Moereels ensured that the parkland surrounding his home was very much part of the interior.**

Right **If your loft has no external space, bring the outdoors in by using natural found objects in the decoration of the interior.**

A croissant and a coffee in the morning; an impromptu dinner for 12 friends; 60 people for drinks on a Saturday night; a lazy Sunday brunch for two. A pleasurable, social and informal part of life, there is nothing formulaic about the way we eat, so why make do with a formulaic eating space? Instead of single rooms for separate functions – cooking, dining, entertaining – we need one open, flexible, informal, multipurpose space where we can do it all, and a loft gives you the chance to create it.

eating

Think about how you use your kitchen and devise a layout that will work for you. Put it in the centre of the living zone (on a platform if you like) and leave it open to the eating area and living space, so it becomes like the bridge of a ship, a place from which you can see everything. Or tuck it to one side of your loft and separate it with an island of units or a curvy worktop. Don't be afraid to make it massively functional with a giant cooker, an expansive work surface and a big, big fridge. Ex-industrial spaces cry out for catering-scale kitchen equipment and a utilitarian look is all the rage. Make it practical and user-friendly, with a durable floor, well-targeted lighting and lots and lots of storage.

Your dining area should be functional and flexible with a table that is big enough for parties but simple enough to work at, and chairs you could sit in all day. Make it an extension of the kitchen and create a visual link between the two by using the same tones or materials. Although practicality is key, that doesn't mean you have to go short on comfort or colour.

Previous page **Using sleek surfaces and a dash of colour, you can create a pared-down eating area that is functional as well as good-looking.**

This page **Connect the kitchen to the rest of your space by filling it with things you like, whether it is a sculptural bowl or some brilliant glassware.**

Above left **By covering a wall with blue-toned oblong tiles, the owners of this London loft defined their kitchen area while leaving it open to the main space. They also created an ingenious, inexpensive dining table out of an old hospital trolley and a new plane of wood.**

Above right **A touch of kitsch and colour will add instant personality to the rawest of loft spaces.**

Left **Here, there is no division between the kitchen and dining area. The two functions are simply contained within one minimal streamlined space.**

165

working

The study, a room that once comprised no more than a desk, a chair and a bookcase, is not what it was. At the end of the twentieth century it has had to take on a new, far more vital role as more and more of us are using our homes to work from. Indeed, what we want today is not a study but a work station – a change in terminology that alone expresses our new expectations of this home-cum-work space.

While we want this new kind of study area to be supremely functional and equipped with the latest technology, we also need it to slot as unobtrusively as possible into our home. In a loft with an open-plan layout, you can't simply shut your office away, so do all you can to make your working space part of your interior by choosing office furniture that is functional but that also fits in with the rest of your furnishings.

Although you can set up office anywhere in a loft (at the dining table, for example), it makes more sense to set your work space slightly apart from your living space, if only to avoid you thinking about work when you should be relaxing and vice versa. This doesn't mean building walls but simply partitioning your interior to give some sort of separation – a sliding door, perhaps, or some fabric drapes. This way, you can keep the place where you work free of domestic clutter.

Your home office doesn't have to be big (some loft dwellers have used large cupboards to great effect), but whatever the size, certain general principles apply. Install good task lighting (particularly if it is situated at the back of your space) and choose flexible furniture. Opting for a self-contained work unit on wheels or a coloured filing cabinet that would look good anywhere, for example, will make it easy to transform what is your work space by day into an extra bedroom by night.

Previous page **Here, the working area is contained along one wall of the interior but kept open to the living space so that it is quiet but not cut off.**

Opposite top **Dark wood furniture gives a business-like feel to this home office.**

Opposite far left and left **This Belgian stylist converted the whole of his ground floor into a studio that is flooded with natural light.**

Above **Given the right kind of furniture, some efficient lighting and a will to work, you can turn any unused corner of your loft into a mini home office.**

Right **To get the most out of your work space, create an efficient filing and storage system. These swivelling wooden boxes are brilliantly functional – and they look good, too.**

bathing

In a loft, your bathroom doesn't have to be an
afterthought, squeezed into a dark space the size of a
cupboard; it can be whatever you want it to be – big or
small, grand or rustic, natural or high-tech. Create a
bathroom that will suit your needs: somewhere clean-lined
and functional for a quick shower or an intimate, indulgent
haven if you like to wallow in the bath for hours.

Previous page **Whether you like Victorian splendour or a raw and industrial look, create a bathroom that, above all, works for you.**

Left **Semi-enclosed by planes of frosted glass, this streamlined shower in a Belgian loft is both self-contained and part of the main living space.**

Below left **A sculptural basin adds a rustic touch to a sleek London loft.**

Below **Unfussy in the extreme, this bathroom has a monastic feel.**

In a loft, a bathroom doesn't have to be linear; consider creating a curving or circular space. Think of unconventional ways to screen it from view – frosted or coloured glass, for example, will let in the light (particularly useful if your bathroom is at the back of the loft) but retain your modesty; a folding wall or sliding door will allow you to open up the room as and when you feel like it. Alternatively, you can leave your bathroom open to your bedroom, hidden simply by a freestanding panel of wall; or do without walls altogether and place your bath out in the centre of your living space (but make sure you have somewhere to store all that bathroom clutter).

As far as materials are concerned, anything goes as long as it is water-resistant – wood, stone, recycled plastic, stainless steel. Simply choose whichever appeals and don't be afraid to introduce strong colour. Even in a modishly monochrome interior, a bathroom can get away with being brilliant. Try bold rubber tiles on the floor or line a shower with vivid fibreglass.

Whatever option you choose, make sure the place where you bathe is not right next to the kitchen. Cooking smells travel – particularly in an open-plan space – and while some may be enticing (bacon on a Sunday morning, fresh coffee and baking bread), others may not. If all else fails, get an extractor fan and light those scented candles.

Above **Bathrooms can take colour. Here, blue mosaics offset a raw concrete wall, and a shower brings a dash of vivid yellow to a neutral loft space.**

Below **Simple and natural materials work best with water, so anything from smooth stone to aromatic teak will make a bathroom both look and feel good.**

sleeping

The most private and personal part of any interior, the place where you sleep should be somewhere you feel absolutely at ease. You will spend more or less half your life there, after all, so make it a cocoon of comfort and tranquillity; a sensual sanctuary from the strains of urban life; somewhere to chill out at the end of a hard-working day. If your living area is edgy and industrial, change the tone in your sleeping area with calming colours and soft textures.

Previous page **In a loft, the area where you sleep should be the ultimate comfort zone, so turn your bedroom into a sanctuary by minimizing clutter and maximizing texture.**

Above left **Separating the bedroom from the main living space with a simple curtain gives you the flexibility to go open-plan again whenever you like.**

Above **Muted colours and soft carpet will do much to increase the comfort factor.**

Left **A floor-to-ceiling headboard-cum-screen makes an innovative en-suite solution.**

Position your bedroom with care. If you have divided your loft, place the bedroom as far as you can from the hustle and bustle of your living area and kitchen. Tuck it at the back, under a mezzanine if you have one, so it can become be a quiet and secret space to retreat to. If your interior is open-plan, provide privacy with a screen or flexible partition. Put the bedroom within easy reach of the bathroom or combine the two in one expansive space. Create a divide, if you wish, with a freestanding panel of wall or frosted glass and make sure you have effective ventilation.

Build as much storage as you need into the structure so you can keep furniture to a minimum. Some of the best loft bedrooms have just a giant bed that incorporates everything from the side table to the lighting. Go all out for comfort. Choose flooring that feels good underfoot, curtains or blinds that diffuse the light and a bed big enough to spend all day in. And maximize those mod cons, so you can have music, lighting and warmth at the flick of a switch.

Above **A series of soft, diaphanous curtains will not only screen a sleeping area but bring an element of fluidity to the harshest ex-industrial space.**

Left **Grand furniture can work brilliantly in a loft. Here, a carved wood bed and chair, upholstered in Vivienne Westwood fabric, add a dash of glamour to an ex-office space.**

5

impact
& influences

the changing home
new developments

The loft gave us **open** space just when we needed it; it gave us **flexible** furniture to fill it with; and, **best of all**, it gave us a way to be **modern** without being a modernist.

the changing home

In the last half of the twentieth century there has been a significant shift in attitude towards the home. While once we rated property by the number of rooms it had, these days we assess a living space less on its physical features than its abstract qualities. We want light. We want unfettered space. We want somewhere without dividing walls; a multipurpose place where we can cook, eat and entertain simultaneously. Today, open-plan has shed its hippie image to become the latest architectural cliché.

The reasons for this change are largely social. When the tools of contemporary life – the washing machine, the dishwasher, even the office space – can fit in a cupboard, there is no need for a laundry, a pantry or a study to accommodate them. When we are happy to sit and chat with our guests as we cook, we no longer want to divide the dining room and the kitchen. When we don't employ a cook, a maid or a tutor, we have no need for separate rooms to put them in.

The end-of-the-century desire for open-plan – or at least, partially open-plan – living is thus a response to a change in lifestyle, but the loft itself has also played an instrumental part. The ideal arena in which to try out a new, more informal way of life, the loft has added momentum to the general movement. Encouraged by its example and success, people living in conventional housing all around the world are knocking down walls to give their homes more space, more light, more flexibility. As British architect Duncan Chapman admits: 'We are arguably chopping up terraced houses much more radically than we might have done without the loft experience.'

the furnishing evolution

Furthermore, lofts have not just had an impact on the shape of our homes but also on what we put inside them. Catering to the demands of streamlined, open-plan space instead of individual rooms, furniture has become increasingly adaptable and equivocal, embracing modular forms that can be used anywhere and changed at whim: the table that turns into a chest, for example, or the storage boxes that can be piled up to make impromptu shelving. Loft-style in essence, such designs have now become part of the general lexicon of modern furniture and are just as popular in conventional homes as in lofts themselves.

So, too, with industrial materials. Although they, like open-plan living, were not discovered by the loft dweller (it was the modern architects of the 1930s and 1940s who first brought concrete, steel and glass out of the factory and into the home), what the loft has done is to sanction the use of them in more mainstream living spaces. You don't need to be an out-and-out modernist to invest in a catering-style stainless-steel cooker or an aluminium floor, for example. You don't even need to live in a loft. The industrial look has become an aesthetic in its own right and is now exploited in all sorts of homes around the world.

It could be said, then, that the loft has simply acted as an enabler of trends that were already under way. It gave us open-plan space just when we realized that the dining room had become defunct. It gave us flexible furniture to fill it with. It showed us, most significantly of all, a way to be modern without being a modernist. It is little wonder that people are adopting its ideas and aesthetics en masse.

Previous page and opposite **'Light, space and nature are the basis of the design,' says architect Pascal van der Kelen of his low, white modernist house on the outskirts of Antwerp.** **Laid out geometrically in Bauhaus style, its rooms flow freely into each other, with half-walls providing partitions between them without disrupting the openness of the space.**

new developments

Most significantly, the commercial and social success of the loft has highlighted the demand for a more modern approach to housing generally and made even the conventional building companies sit up and take notice. A consequent change in development is particularly evident in Britain, where good modern housing has been virtually nonexistent up until now (a circumstance which, ironically, encouraged the trend for loft-living in the first place).

British house builder Barratt, for example – renowned for the retrospective, neoclassical bias of its building – has, in its more recent developments, created homes that embrace modernity, both outside and in. 'There's definitely been a change; a feeling that it's about time we started looking forward in this country rather than back,' commented a London estate agent. 'For years people rejected it, but … it has suddenly become acceptable and it's moving out of the Soho and Clerkenwell loft communities into other areas.'*

As Sydney-based architect Ian Moore says: 'In the twenty-first century, space and environmental wellbeing will be a luxury for everyone, so as we approach the millennium, why build houses that look and function like houses from the last century?'** The loft has

Artists Elizabeth Ogilvie and Robert Callender turned an old cinema on the shores of Fife in Scotland (below left) into a brilliantly lit living space and a vast studio. Their seaside 'loft' is filled with wooden boats (below right), objects salvaged from the beach and their own artworks, such as Callender's Coastal Collection (opposite). The pieces look like sea salvage but are actually made from painted papier-mâché, cardboard and sculpted wood.

shown us a prototype for a new kind of living space that meets our end-of-the-century needs and, as lofts themselves reach saturation point as possible conversions in cities worldwide dry up, we will see a significant rise in loft-style housing, in new homes that put light and space at the top of the list rather than period detail.

the future of the loft

Given its pervasive influence, loft-living is not a fad that will fade away. The Western world has never had more disposable income and, as architect Duncan Chapman explains, while notions of progress remain bound up with materiality, developing one's own designer habitat will be one of the choices available to increasingly more people. 'It won't just be designer lampshades for everyone,' he says, 'but homes, too.' Above all, the popularity of lofts has left us with a legacy of millions of new urban living spaces, which may change hands and evolve over the years to come but which have transformed the face of cities all around the world forever.

The studio is 75 feet (23 metres) wide and 66 feet (20 metres) long, so Callender's vast collection of salvaged boats and driftwood can easily be accommodated.

Opposite **Ogilivie's work –
lyrical sculptures made
from glass and steel –
look perfectly at home
in this light, open gallery-
like space.**

Left **The combination
of poetic sculptures and
carefully placed natural
seaside forms makes the
whole interior look like a
work of art.**

Below **The open-plan living
space right at the top of
the building is filled with
a minimum of furniture.**

resources

fabrics & wall coverings

Barsouv
91 Orchard St.
New York, NY 10002
212.925.3400

Circle Fabrics
263 W. 38th St.
New York, NY 10018
212.719.5153

Donghia
979 3rd Ave.
New York, NY 10022
212.935.3712
(to the trade)

J. Robert Scott
500 N. Oak St.
Inglewood, CA 90302
310.680.4300
(to the trade)

Nobilis, Inc.
973 3rd Ave.
New York, NY 10022
212.980.1177
(to the trade)

metal work

Edelman Metalworks
9 State St.
Danbury, CT 06810
203.744.7331

Jeff Mase
39 9th Ave.
New York, NY 10014
212.929.1289

leathergoods

Libra Leather, Inc.
259 W. 30th St.
New York, NY 10001
212.695.3114

Renar
68 Spring St.
New York, NY 10012
212.349.2075

window treatments, curtains & blinds

Allstate Glass
85 Kenmare St.
New York, NY 10012
212.226.2517

George Molina
100 Emerson Pl.
Brooklyn, NY 11205
718.789.3190
Curtains, drapes, upholstery

flooring

American Olean Tile Company
100 Cannon Ave.
Lansdale, PA 19446
215.855.1111

Architectural Systems
150 W. 25th St.
New York, NY 10001
212.206.1730
Multipurpose flooring

DWF (Designer Wood Flooring)
446 W. 38th St.
New York, NY 10018
212.971.0226

Kentucky Wood Floor
P.O. Box 33726
Louisville, KY 40232
800.235.5235

Perfect Circle Studios
64 Jay St.
Brooklyn, NY 11201
718.643.0244
Stainless steel flooring tiles

decorative paint & materials

Bendheim Glass
122 Hudson St.
New York, NY 10013
212.226.6370
Glass and glass cubes

Cesar Color Inc.
4625 S. 32nd St.
Phoenix, AZ 85040
602.243.1434
Glass

John Depp
41–40 38th St.
Long Island City, NY 11101
718.784.8500
Glass, mirror

Foro
140 3rd St.
Brooklyn, NY 11231
718.852.2322
Marble

Fresco
324 Lafayette St.
New York, NY 10012
212.966.0676

Joanne Hudson Assoc. Ltd
The Marketplace Design Center
2400 Market St., Suite 310
Philadelphia, PA 19103
800.217.7931

Renfrow Tile
1822 Sunnyside Ave.
Charlotte, NC 28204
704.334.6811
Marble, glass tile

Chris Townley
208 Bowery
New York, NY 10012
212.941.1606
Plaster

lighting

Cooper Lighting
P.O. Box 4446
Houston, TX 77210
713.739.5400

Donzella 20th Century
17 White St.
New York, NY 10013
212.965.8919

Flos, Inc.
200 McKay Rd.
Huntington Station, NY 11746
516.549.2745
(to the trade)

Fontana Arte
8807 Beverly Blvd.
Los Angeles, CA 90048
310.247.9933

Ideas & Products
31 S. 5th Ave.
Tucson, AZ 85716
520.791.9267

Lighting By Gregory
158 Bowery
New York, NY 10012
212.226.1276

Luceplan USA
315 Hudson St.
New York, NY 10013
212.691.8263
(to the trade)

Urban Archeology Co.
143 Franklin St.
New York, NY 10013
212.431.4646

Villa Lighting
1218 S. Vandeventer
St. Louis, MO 63110
800.325.0963

kitchen & bath

AF Supply
22 W. 21 St.
New York, NY 10010
212.243.5400

Bowery Discount Hardware
& Restaurant Supply
105 Bowery
New York, NY 10002
212.966.6375
Kitchen

The Chicago Faucet Co.
2100 S. Nuclear Dr.
Des Plaines, IL 60018
847.803.5000

George Taylor Specialties
100 Hudson St.
New York, NY 10013
212.226.5369

JADO Bath & Hardware
Mfg. Co.
1690 Calle Quetzal
Camarillo, CA 93011
805.482.2666

Kohler Co.
Design Center
101 Upper Rd.
Kohler, WI 53044
920.457.3699

Waterworks
469 Broome St.
New York, NY 10013
212.966.0605
Bathroom

furniture & accessories

ABC Carpet & Home
888 Broadway
New York, NY 10003
212.473.3000

Aero
132 Spring St.
New York, NY 10012
212.966.1500

BDDW
8 Rivington St.
New York, NY 10002
212.228.7322
Furniture, lighting, design

Coconut Company
131 Greene St.
New York, NY 10012
212.539.1940

Domestic Furniture
6150 Wilshire Blvd.
Los Angeles, CA 90036
323.936.8206

Form & Function
95 Vandam St.
New York, NY 10013
212.414.1800

Global Table
187 Sullivan St.
New York, NY 10012
212.431.5839

Holly Hunt
979 3rd Ave.
New York, NY 10022
212.755.6555
(to the trade)

Jet Age Studio
250 Oak St.
San Francisco, CA 94102
415.864.1950

Knoll
105 Wooster St.
New York, NY 10012
212.343.4102
(to the trade)

Lin Weinberg
84 Wooster St.
New York, NY 10012
212.219.3022

Dennis Miller Associates
306 E. 61st St.
New York, NY 10021
212.355.4550
(to the trade)

M2L
979 3rd Ave.
New York, NY 10022
212.832.8222
(to the trade)

Modern Living
8775 Beverly Blvd.
Los Angeles, CA 90048
310.657.8557

Moss
146 Greene St.
New York, NY 10012
212.219.3022

Pucci International
44 W. 18th St.
New York, NY 10011
212.633.0452

Marc O. Rabun
Art & Antiques
115 Crosby St.
New York, NY 10012
212.226.5053

Totem Design
71 Franklin St.
New York, NY 10013
212.463.8910

Troy
138 Greene St.
New York, NY 10012
212.941.4777

280 Modern
280 Layfayette St.
New York, NY 10012
212.941.5825

Vintage Modern Gallery
1515 N. Central Ave.
Phoenix, AZ 85004
602.462.5790

Wyeth
151 Franklin St.
New York, NY 10013
212.925.5278

architectural salvage

Demolition Depot
216 E. 125th St
New York, NY 10035
212.860.1138

Renovator's Supply
Renovator's Old Mill
Millers Falls, MA 01349
800.659.2211

Wooden Nickel Antiques
1410 Central Parkway
Cincinnati, OH 45210
513.241.2985

carpet & rugs

Dolma
417 Lafayette, 2nd Fl.
New York, NY 10003
212.460.5525

Einstein Moomjy Inc.
150 E. 58th St.
New York, NY 10155
212.758.0980

Mark Shilen
109 Greene St.
New York, NY 10012
212.925.3394

websites

www.interiorinternet.com
www.furniture.com
www.internetdesigncenter.com
www.lampa.com
www.totemdesign.com
www.industrial-home.com
www.rabidhome.com

index

acknowledgments

The publishers would like to thank the following sources for their kind permission to reproduce the pictures in this book:

Peter Aaron/Holley New York 17t
Aurelia PR 109
Babylon Design 80–1
Michael Banks 90, 92, 93
Henry Bourne 1, 40, 41, 43, 51, 70, 128, 129, 132, 134, 142, 156, 157, 178–9, 181, 190 (*Elle Decoration* no. 52: 40, 41, 42, 132; *Elle Decoration* no. 58: 51; *Elle Decoration* no. 65: 134)
Edra spa 148–9, 150, 151t
Elizabeth Crompton-Batt PR 52/
P Harmer 88, 89
Peter Gidal 15
David Giles 46, 47, 173tr
Richard Glover/Millennium Images 25, 26, 27, 30–1, 38, 39, 62–3, 175
Rene Gonkel (stylist Jeanne van Andel) 44, 45
Mark Guard Architects 94
Michael Harding, Carlton Books Ltd 32, 33, 107, 114–15, 133, 135b, 136, 139b, 144t, 145, 146, 147, 152, 153t, 154, 164t, 169l, 176tl, 188–9
Falk Hirdes 54–5, 96–7, 98–9, 100, 101
Interior Archive/Fritz von der Schulenburg, Paola Navone (architect) 104, 105, 144b (caption source *Elle Decoration* no. 44)
David Loftus 158, 161, 182, 183, 184–5, 186, 187 (*Elle Decoration* no. 72)
Ray Main 28, 29, 64, 65, 86, 108, 113, 122, 123, 137, 153b, 155, 169r
Nadia Mackenzie 56, 57, 141, 165tr, 177b
Ocean Shopping 151b
Powell-Tuck Associates/Henry Bourne 48–9, 82, 83, 84, 85, 176tr
Ed Reeve 130, 131
Laura Resen 18, 19, 20, 21 (caption source *Elle Decoration* no. 46)
Claudio Silvestrin Ltd (lighting artist Adam Barker Mill) 71
Thomas Stewart 72–3, 112–13, 140, 143, 163, 172bl, 192
Verne/Claire Bataille and Paul Ibens (architects and owners) 110t, 111 (*Elle Decoration* no. 71)
Verne/Manu and Ann Demuynck (owners), Wim de Cuyver (architect) 6, 7, 110b, 126, 127, 159, 162–3, 164br, 168bl, 168br, 171, 177tr, (*Elle Decoration* no. 63)
Verne/Els Lybeert and Thomas Siffer (owners), Wim De Puydt (architect) 4, 5, 66, 67, 68, 69, 116, 117, 118, 120–1, 172t (*Elle Decoration* no. 80)
Verne/Jan Moereels (owner), Jo Crepain (architect) 2–3, 34, 35, 36, 37, 65, 160, 173tl (*Elle Decoration* no. 74)
Verne/Nathalie van Reeth (architect and owner) 8, 11, 22–3, 60–1, 135t, 164bl, 165b, 166, 167, 168t, 172br, 173b, 174 (*Elle Decoration* no. 78)
Verne/Katleen and Joris Van Zandtweghe (owners; Katleen, architect) 102–3, 124, 125, 139t (*Elle Decoration* no. 74)
Richard Waite 12, 13, 16, 17b, 58–9, 74, 75, 76–7, 78, 165tl, 170, 176b

Special thanks to:
Owen at Mainstream Photography
Verne

Every effort has been made to acknowledge correctly and contact the source and/or copyright holder of each picture, and Carlton Books Limited apologises for any unintentional errors or omissions which will be corrected in future editions of this book.

authors' acknowledgments

Thanks to everyone who allowed us to publish photographs of their homes. Harry Handelsman and the team at Manhattan Loft Corporation; Colin Serlin of London Buildings; Piers Gough of CZWG; Duncan Chapman of Circus Architects; Mark Guard and Jonathan Bell of Mark Guard Architects; John Pawson; David Rosen of Pilcher Hershman; Andrew Hanson of HM2; Marti Kappell; Jane Tankard and Steve Bowkett … for their time, help and advice. Clive, Ella, India and Müge for infinite patience and huge support.

sources

The Book of Lofts, Suzanne Slesin and Stafford Cliff (Thames and Hudson, 1999).
Lofts in Italy, Paola Gallo and Silvio San Pietro (Edizioni L'Archivolto, 1998).
Back to the Centre, a study by the Royal Institute of Chartered Surveyors, September 1998.

credits

(marked * throughout the text)
Page 23: source *The Book of Lofts*, Suzannze Slesin and Stafford Cliff (Thames and Hudson, 1999).
Page 28: source Joe Joseph whose article in *The Times* on 2 April 1994 proved very helpful.
Page 35: David Putnam, December 1994 and quoted in Manhattan Loft Corporation's Bankside brochure.
Page 38: first quoted by Peter Silverton, *You* magazine.
Page 73: first quoted, *Elle Decoration* no. 62.
Page 183: quoted by Christine Webb in an article in *The Times* on 6 September 1997.
Page 183: first quoted, *Elle Decoration* no. 62.